HOW TO DIE

HOW

RAY ROBERTSON

TO DIE

A Book About Being Alive

BIBLIOASIS
WINDSOR, ONTARIO

FIRST EDITION

Library and Archives Canada Cataloguing in Publication

Title: How to die : a book about being alive / Ray Robertson.
Names: Robertson, Ray, 1966- author.
Description: Includes bibliographical references.
Identifiers: Canadiana (print) 20190220317 | Canadiana (ebook)
    20190220325 | ISBN 9781771960946
    (softcover) | ISBN 9781771960953 (ebook)
Subjects: LCSH: Robertson, Ray, 1966-—Anecdotes. | LCSH: Death. | LCSH:
    Death—Psychological
    aspects. | LCSH: Life.
Classification: LCC BD444 .R63 2020 | DDC 128/.5—dc23

Edited by Daniel Wells
Copy-edited by Allana Amlin
Cover and interior designed by Ingrid Paulson

Published with the generous assistance of the Canada Council for the Arts, which last year invested $153 million to bring the arts to Canadians throughout the country, and the financial support of the Government of Canada. Biblioasis also acknowledges the support of the Ontario Arts Council (OAC), an agency of the Government of Ontario, which last year funded 1,709 individual artists and 1,078 organizations in 204 communities across Ontario, for a total of $52.1 million, and the contribution of the Government of Ontario through the Ontario Book Publishing Tax Credit and Ontario Creates.

PRINTED AND BOUND IN CANADA

CONTENTS

Tom Noyes and Miles Wilson

and

Mara Korkola

What are days for?
Day are where we live.
They come, they wake us
Time and time over.
They are to be happy in:
Where can we live but days?
—Philip Larkin, "Days"

Que sais-je?
—Michel de Montaigne

INTRODUCTION

Someone once asked me if I was ever tempted to revisit a character or a storyline from one of my novels. I could honestly say I hadn't, that it sounded like work, something I've tried hard my entire life to avoid. It also sounded boring, which, for me, is even worse. How can the reader be expected to care if the author doesn't?

This changed after I wrote *Why Not? Fifteen Reasons to Live*, a collection of essays completed after enduring a deep depression brought on by finishing a long, difficult novel amidst the debilitating symptoms of obsessive-compulsive disorder, a disease I've suffered from all of my adult life and which tends to manifest itself most perniciously when I've embarked upon an engrossing project. (If nothing else, it's a reminder of life's ongoing irony: what tends to make me happiest also has the capacity to make me sick.) *How to Die: A Book About Being Alive* isn't a sequel to *Why Not? Fifteen Reasons to Live*—a better diet, more exercise, and the correct dosage of the right medication have helped me remain as psychologically healthy as possible—but, rather, a continuation of the conversation begun in the latter book's final chapter: Death. A conversation with whom? With myself, of course.

That I graduated with High Distinction with a degree in philosophy says less about my analytical reasoning skills or deep knowledge of any particular thinker or branch of philosophy than it does about my desire at the end of my undergraduate career to complete my degree so I could do something else. Simply put, philosophy—which from as far back as high school had seemed the zenith of human activities—had become a bore (there's that word again). There'd been plenty of inspired and inspiring books encountered along the way—Pascal's *Pensées*, Simone Weils' *Gravity and Grace*, Martin Buber's *I and Thou*, nearly everything written by Nietzsche—but, I came to learn, these works and others like them weren't considered "real" philosophy by the academic community. Instead, they were dismissively lumped together as "wisdom literature": at best, entertaining *belles lettres*; at worst, artsy-fartsy blather and bluster. A "real" philosopher was someone like Hegel, who, like the majority of his professorial brethren, wrote for other professors in a language seemingly created to deter comprehension about subjects as far removed from the everyday philosophical questions and concerns of most human beings as the ugly, ungainly style they employed was from lucid, illuminating prose. As it is with music, so it is with philosophy: if it doesn't swing, it's hard to understand the words. Or care.

One of those writers of "wisdom literature" I discovered during these years was Montaigne, someone I continued to enthusiastically read long after I'd decided that fiction was a better (and much more enjoyable) way of taking reality's temperature. Pascal, Weil, Buber, Nietzsche, et al. were almost always interesting and often eloquent, but there was usually the unmistakable imprint of argumentation on their work. Since they were, after all, philosophers, this was understandable, but Montaigne was a different kind of reading experience. Although he offered opinions on virtually every subject imaginable (drunkenness, mortality, reading, sleep, friendship, anger, virtue, the art of discussion, experience, fame, pedantry, idleness, vanity, praying, cowardice, et cetera), these ideas weren't the only fruit of his labours. Often, they were the least compelling part. Montaigne was born and remained a Catholic, but his ruminations on religion and humankind's place in the universe, for example, were just that: an unflappable, unhurried exploration of every aspect of whatever subject happened to interest him, whether that led him into profundity, confusion, or even contradiction. Montaigne's biographer and one of his finest translators, Donald Frame, described Montaigne's style as "free, oral, informal, personal, concrete, luxuriant in images, organic and spontaneous in order, ranging from the epigrammatic to the rambling and associative." One of the many pleasures of reading Montaigne is the sense that one is not so much reading a book as simply listening to an amiable, amusing, intellectually ecumenical human being thinking aloud about a variety of subjects that interest him, ultimate conclusions and logical consistency be damned. As befits the originator of the modern essay, Montaigne wrote foremost to find out what *he* thought, and his readers are invited along to listen in while he does so. Maybe best of all, Montaigne is good company.

He was also a dedicated amateur classicist, the very best kind of aficionado (he read and reread Horace and Cicero and Virgil and Ovid and Lucretius and others not to become or to appear learned, but because these ancient authors continued to stimulate and sustain him). His famous tower in Bordeaux, where he retired to ponder life and compose his essays, were packed with volumes by these cherished authors for the same reason that the home of the early eighteenth-century

Scottish poet James Thomson was similarly stocked: "To cheer the gloom / There studious let me sit, / And hold high converse with the mighty dead." Montaigne's work is embroidered with the best that had been thought and said by these mighty dead, and he himself anticipated a possible objection to his literary method: "[S]omeone might say of me that I have here only made up a bunch of other people's flowers, having furnished nothing of my own but the thread to tie them." But Montaigne's point of view is rarely overwhelmed by these other voices, which only serve to embellish and illuminate the essayist's own thoughts and feelings. Nearly five hundred years of writers who have been inspired by, and attempted to emulate, his method may not have been as successful (myself included, utilizing many favourite long-deceased authors of my own who weren't even born when Montaigne was alive and composing his essays), but that's one of the reasons one keeps writing. Maybe next time you'll get it right. Or at least closer to what it's supposed to be.

If *How to Die: A Book About Being Alive* is supposed to *be* anything, it's an examination of death (what it is and how we think about it) counterbalanced by a spirited rebuttal from life. When I told a friend I was writing this book, she replied, "What do you know about death?" (Meaning, I believe, both of my parents were still alive and my wife and I were healthy and happy.) All I could think to answer was, "As much as anybody who hasn't died yet, I guess." Additionally, an odd thing happens once one reaches the mid-century mark: people start to die. Not just any people, either, but people you know well and sometimes even love: colleagues, friends, family. And people you don't know but have known all your life anyway: the sports and musical heroes, the movie actors and newsmakers of our youth and early adulthood, most of whom, even before they die, slowly fade from public consciousness (only to be replaced by new, younger icons who will, in time, endure their own eclipse as well.) Favourite restaurants and bars and businesses, too, begin to disappear with regularity, along with things less brick-and-mortar tangible but no less significant. When I moved to Toronto thirty-five years ago (35? No, it can't be, do the math again—wow, yeah, 35), Toronto meant Queen Street West second-hand book buying and dive-bar slumming and Citytv; it meant Maple Leaf Gardens and the Brunswick House; it meant seven (count 'em, seven) repertory theatres. Now, what used to be Queen Street Cool is chiefly a shopping destination for 905ers visiting the city for the afternoon, Citytv is a media conglomerate's neutered facsimile of what it once proudly, independently was, Maple Leaf Gardens is a

Loblaws, and the adored Brunny—scene of so many Bacchanalian stunts and shenanigans—is a Rexall, and most people I know (myself included) get their movies on Netflix or via other streaming services, eliminating the need to ever leave the house. No doubt there are new second-hand bookstores and charmingly sleazy bars, new ways the city is electronically connected and sees itself, new ways of being what it means to be a Torontonian, but it's unlikely I would know about them. Why would I? It's not really my city anymore. One generation passeth away, another generation cometh, and ain't that a drag.

The question isn't, then, why think or write about extinction (our own and everyone and everything else's), but—pardon the pun—why not? Not that my every thought on the subject will prove agreeable or even appear entirely convincing to everyone. (As Montaigne reminded himself—and us—"What do I know?") And that's a good thing. If I'm not making some people angry, I'm probably not doing my job. And if it's true that we're disposed to like people who like us, writers don't—or shouldn't—like readers who agree with everything they write. A book—particularly a book such as this—is a conversation, first between the author and him or herself, then between the writer and the reader. And when people converse, sometimes they disagree. And sometimes it's out of such disagreements that we come to a better, clearer understanding of what we actually do believe. So, for instance, although atheism is to me only slightly less illogical than theism (and organized religion itself, as Mary McCarthy argued, is only "good for good people" because, for the rest, "it is too great a temptation—a temptation to the deadly sins of pride and anger, chiefly, but one might also add sloth"), and agnosticism the only rational response to a multitude of important metaphysical questions, I wouldn't have come to these admittedly debatable beliefs without the aid of the work of a wealth of wise theologians. My undergraduate degree was a double major (philosophy and religious studies), and Christian existentialists such as Gabriel Marcel and Nicholas Berdyaev and Sam Keen and Harvey Cox (as well as the aforementioned Weil and Buber) were almost as important to my intellectual development (if far less aesthetically satisfying) as the titanic Nietzsche (who, by the way, was the son and grandson of Lutheran pastors). "Do I contradict myself?" Whitman asked in "Song of Myself." Of course I do. And you know what? Again, like Whitman, that's okay: "I am large, I contain multitudes."

I also have a tattoo of a skull and roses on my right forearm. I got it because I'm a (Grateful) Deadhead, but also because it's such an apposite image for existence. Encircling the outline of the skull with black holes for eyes is a garland of fresh red roses. Death in life. Life in death. If there's a thesis to *How to Die: A Book About Being Alive* it's that, if we gain a better understanding of what death is, we'll also know more of what life consists. Montaigne claimed that "My trade and my art is living." Nice work if you can get it. May we all be so profitably occupied.

PART ONE

PART ONE

No one forgets their first time. It's the *other* first time—the one that darkens the mind rather than delights the body—that isn't always as instantly memorable. But it's there—somewhere—along with the initial recognition that our parents aren't the wisest, most powerful people in the world who will always be there to protect us, that people don't have to love us back just because we want them to, and that the game of life doesn't come with a set of inviolable rules that everyone is obliged to follow in the interest of fair play. Not that it's difficult to understand why we don't always remember the precise time and place when we first became aware, however dimly, of death. That everyone is going to die. That *I'm* going to die. Human beings tend to hide from what hurts. Or at least attempt to. But Grandma's funeral or the family pet's last visit to the veterinarian or a flattened frog in the middle of the street remind us of what we try to forget but never entirely can.

Novelists aren't good at much. Busy describing how the world lives, there isn't much time or inclination left over to do much worldly living oneself. But remembering things—in particular, the seemingly inconsequential but singularly significant minutiae of daily existence—is an occupational necessity. I remember my first whiff of nothingness. Wrote about it in my novel *What Happened Later*:

Let's go around, I said.

An August afternoon Sunday when I was five, an idling '69 Buick Skylark with power windows but no air conditioning, a train that wouldn't end like Christmas will never come and summer vacation will go on forever. I was hot and bored and thirsty and there was cold pop at home on the bottom shelf of the bar fridge in the basement.

We can't go around, my dad said.

Why not?

Because they'll put you in a box and put you in the ground and they won't let you out.

I thought about what he said. It didn't make sense. I said the only sensible thing I could think of.

But you'd let me out, I said.

My father leaned against the steering wheel and craned his neck left, looked as far down the railroad track as he could. Sweat rivered down the back of his neck. He looked in the rear-view mirror to make sure there was no one behind us; put the car in reverse and gave the steering wheel a sharp tug to the right. We weren't going to wait around anymore. Finally, we were moving. Looking in the mirror again, this time at me in the back seat:

I don't want to see you fooling around when there's a train coming, he said.

I won't.

You either stand back and wait for it to go by, or you walk around to where it isn't, you hear me?

I know.

Hey?

I'll wait for it or walk around.

My mother sucked a last suck from her Player's Light and pulled the ashtray out of the dash, crushed out her cigarette on the metal lip. It was full of mashed cigarette butts crowned with red lipstick kisses.

Because when they put you in that box in the ground, boy, that's it, nobody can help you.

But, I wanted to say.

But I didn't say anything. And my dad—I waited—he didn't say anything either.

Not that I consider myself as having been particularly thanatosophically precocious; death-consciousness simply comes to some early, while others don't attend their first class in *Introduction to Eventual Personal Extinction* (a.k.a. *Death 101*) until they're well on their way to graduating from life. When I asked a friend of mine from high school, now a successful dentist in his mid-fifties with a much younger wife and three small children and a vacation home in Arizona neighbouring a private golf course, if he ever thought about his eventual non-existence, he answered, "I'm too busy to think about death." His response might seem glib, even for a dentist with a three handicap, but it's typical of most people's attitude if asked the same question.

And why shouldn't it be? Not just because there are other things more pleasant to contemplate or because considered rumination isn't as common a human activity as, say, envying, lying, or over-eating, but because, as Freud argued, it's virtually impossible for human beings to imagine their own deaths. "Whenever we attempt to do so," he claimed, "we can perceive that we are in fact still present as spectators...At bottom no one believes in his own death...[I]n the unconscious

every one of us is convinced of his own immortality."
And not just when we're young and ontologically
unsophisticated. Consider the seventy-two-year-old
writer William Saroyan's last public words (in a phone
call to the *Associated Press* announcing his terminal
cancer): "Everybody has got to die, but I have always
believed an exception would be made in my case." (Perhaps understanding that we must die, yet not really
believing it, is merely a helpful evolutionary trick, a
pre-programmed delusion that allows us to live more
secure, hence more adventurous lives—and therefore
be happier, more aggressive procreators. It wouldn't be
the first time biology got caught calling the shots.)

But even if we're not psychologically capable of
fully comprehending our own death, we are able to
feel its presence, however dimly sensed or no matter
how imperfectly we might be able to articulate it. Even
without staring directly at the sun, it's possible to
point to its place in the sky. Literature is humankind's
best record of who it is—most everything else is, at best,
either reality-corroding clichés or, at worst, egocentric
self-advertising—and the most compelling evocations
of death in literature (whether in the form of novels,
short stories, poems, memoirs, or essays) approximate
Mallarme's Symbolist poetic dictum: "Paint, not the
object, but the effect it produces." We might not possess

the psychological equipment to take a clear and definitive photograph of death, but, by snapping away at its varied effects, we can know the unknowable a little bit better, just as the mystic doesn't speak directly of "God" but, instead, of God's manifestation in nature, music, or the experience of love.

It's because impression, metaphor, and inference (and their employment in literature) are superior to purely conceptual thinking in disclosing some of death's mystery that philosophers tend to obfuscate more often than illuminate. Art is empirical and therefore the ideal tool for handling something that is understood, to whatever degree, on a primarily experiential level. "No reader who doesn't actually experience, who isn't made to feel … is going to believe anything the … writer merely tells him," Flannery O'Connor counselled. "The first and most obvious characteristic of [good writing] is that it deals with reality through what can be seen, heard, smelt, tasted, and touched."

Even philosophers who make a point of differentiating themselves from other thinkers deemed cripplingly logocentric tend to double death's riddle by obscuring it in a mess of twisted syntax and near-meaningless nouns and verbs. Here's Martin Heidegger taking a crack at the subject with characteristic Heideggerian clarity and linguistic grace: "The existential project of an authentic being-toward-death must thus set forth the factors of such a being which are constitutive for it as an understanding of death—in the sense of being toward this possibility without fleeing it or covering it over." And, yes, many German philosophers do seem to believe that it's a virtue to construct prose that goes down about as well as a tinfoil sandwich, but here's a sample sentence from *Being and Nothingness*, France's most well-known twentieth-century philosopher's, Jean Paul Sartre's, magnum opus: "Death is not my possibility of no longer realizing a presence in the world but rather an always possible nihilation of my possibles which is outside my possibilities." Got that? Have the scales begun to fall from your eyes? One immediately thinks of Friedrich Nietzsche, one German philosopher who did write with perspicuity, elegance, and even (rare for his profession) wit: "They all muddy their waters to make them appear deep." No matter how impressive their academic credentials or how long their list of prized publications, as the nineteenth-century man of letters Jules Renard avowed, "So long as thinkers cannot tell me what life and death are, I shall not give a good god-damn for their thoughts."

More than our opposable thumbs and consequent ability to create such contemporary wonders as Twitter, shoot-and-splatter video games, and reality television, foreknowledge of our own mortality is humankind's defining characteristic. We may not know when we'll die or how or why or what happens afterward, but we do know we *are* going to die. It's ironic, then, that often our first encounter with death is through the loss of the family pet, who, lacking our gift (curse?) of self-consciousness, is denied this bitter wisdom. Our beloved cats and dogs may have felt pain and loss of vitality preceding their expiration, but not anxiety or sadness or fear at their impending annihilation. Those feelings are left for us to experience, often for the first time.

My first pet was a bushy-tailed grey Persian cat named Pepé, as in Pepé Le Pew (she came with the name—we inherited her from an elderly neighbour who couldn't care for her any longer), who died when I was nine years old. Unlike children who are raised on farms and see the life cycle up close on a daily basis ("Don't get attached to the animals, they're not your friends, they're food"), those of us who grow up in suburbia or in the city tend to be shielded from death's glare. One day Pepé seemed to be lying around more than usual and wasn't interested in her toy mouse as much, and the next day, when I came from school, she was gone. My mother told me that she and my father had taken Pepé to the vet because she hadn't been feeling well, and the vet said she was very, very sick, and it would be cruel to let her suffer, so they'd had her put to sleep. It was then that I noticed that her food and water bowls were gone from their usual place on the kitchen floor and that the living room wasn't littered with her balls, toys, and the long piece of silver tinsel she'd claimed as hers from the Christmas tree a couple of months previous. My mother told me that dinner would be ready in about half an hour. We were having pork chops and canned green beans and boiled potatoes.

I'd heard the expression "put to sleep" before, when our next door neighbour's beagle had been euthanized. I was friends with the family's younger brother, who was my age, but it was his older brother by a year who I overheard saying, "I wonder what Molly is dreaming about" when the subject of their recently deceased dog came up. My friend smiled and said, "Squirrels, probably," and his brother smiled too. "Yeah, probably," he said. I didn't know what happened to Pepé or Molly or anyone else's pets once they made their only one-way trip to the veterinarian, but I knew they weren't sleeping. Not what we called *sleeping*, anyway. People who said that their pet "had to be put down" seemed closer to the truth. *Put down* wasn't much more helpful in aiding my understanding of what actually occurred behind the veterinarian's walls, but the polite violence of the phrase felt, uncomfortably, right. Poor Pepé: she'd been put down.

I felt sorry for her, that she wouldn't get to slap at her piece of tinsel again. I felt sorry for me because I wouldn't get to tease her with it again, holding it in front of her face then pulling it away, the way she liked. I missed her because other people's cats weren't her, were different colours and different sizes and didn't like to play the same way—weren't my cat. I felt funny because someone who was here all the time suddenly wasn't anymore. She was just a cat, I knew, but she was Pepé, and now there wasn't a cat called Pepé anymore. It didn't seem fair. It didn't make sense.

The first person I knew who died wasn't someone I knew. Not really. My mother's grandfather died when I was four, a year or so before my almost-epiphany at the train tracks. He lived in a small building behind my grandparents' house—actually, a tarpaper hut no bigger than a large garden shed that lacked running water and its own bathroom—and I only remember, when visiting my grandparents, being aware that outside, out back, there was an old man—a man even older than Grandpa—who lived in a shed. My mother's parents were French-Canadian exiles from the nearby farming community of Paincourt, who'd moved to Chatham looking for better-paying work. I'm not sure they ever found any. My grandfather eventually got a job driving a dump truck for a sand and gravel company, and he and my grandmother rolled their own cigarettes, drank lots of whisky and listened to loud country and western music, and would switch to French whenever they didn't want anyone else to know what they were saying. But the old man in the shed... That's about it: an old man standing in the doorway of a shack while a grey sky pours down cold autumn rain, and even then I'm not sure my mind isn't making something up and calling it a memory merely because I'm trying to come up with one. A quick phone call to my mother reveals that he'd worked the bush in both Quebec and around Paincourt as a hunter's guide, that he could roll a cigarette with one hand, and that they discovered a cyst on his back that turned out to be fatally cancerous. I remember his funeral better than I remember him.

But that's a lie; an exaggeration, at least. I don't remember the ceremony. I don't remember seeing the body (my mother informs me it was an open casket affair). I don't remember watching the corpse being lowered into the ground. I do remember hot rain and steam rising from the road. I remember suits and ties and dresses and the smell of wet polyester. I remember it being too hot inside the car on the ride there and my jacket being itchy. I remember my mother's hairspray smelling like my mother, and the beginning of a small bald spot near the top of my father's head. What else? Nothing else except my mother telling me that I'd been a good boy and we were going home soon. I don't remember crying or complaining or needing any assurance, but I remember feeling happy when my father took off his tie and handed it to my mother who stuffed it into her purse and the car was moving and we really were going home.

Then there are the celebrities, our North American royalty, those who we never knew personally, but whose lives, in some ways, we know better than those of our friends and family and maybe even our own—and whose deaths are almost as equally memorable and meaningful. Each generation has its own "Do you remember when so-and-so died?" and "Where were you when you first heard the news?" For my parents' generation it was the day John F. Kennedy was assassinated. For mine, you never forgot where you were when you heard that Elvis Presley was dead. I was eleven years old and trading baseball cards with Jim Siddle in the basement, the August heat and humidity making it the only cool room in the house. My mother, who kept the local radio station in the kitchen on all day, heard the news first and called down the stairs. "Ray," she said. "Elvis is dead."

There's surprise, of course. How could someone as wealthy and well-known as Elvis really die? But there's more than that. It's not about mourning the music or the films or the good deeds left undone—after all, we still have and will continue to have all of the things that the deceased did that made them well-known to begin with. And unless we're star-obsessed sociopaths, it's obviously not personal sorrow we experience (or imagine we experience). What we miss is the departed's ubiquitous presence. Their (at the risk of committing an act of linguistic ugliness of Heideggerian proportions) thereness. If Elvis can die (Elvis, who Mojo Nixon so sagely sang of in his most well-known tune, "Elvis Is Everywhere"—i.e. in our jeans, in our fast-food, in our parents, in our entire popular culture), then, gulp, I guess we can die too. When the larger-than-life lose their lives, we intuit (as we could never purely logically surmise) that no one is larger than life, that celebrity pantheism is a false religion. Elvis has left the building, folks, and he isn't coming back, no matter how long or hard we wolf whistle and applaud. And so we sit alone in a suddenly very quiet, very empty auditorium whistling "That's All Right Mama" in the dark.

My next funeral I remember better, but not to my credit. A twelve-year-old cousin had died in a swimming accident, a cousin from the side of the family (he was my mother's brother's son) who did things like swing over the Thames River from an old tire hung from a tree before diving into the dirty water below, things I would have never been allowed to do. Worse, I would have never even imagined doing them. My uncle's four kids (all boys) were poor—my uncle worked as a roofer only when he wasn't on a Sudbury Champagne (Canadian Club and ginger ale) bender—and couldn't afford to play year-round organized sports like I did, but when everyone got together a couple of times over the summer for boozy barbecues, it was them, not me, who were quicker, stronger, and better at lawn darts and touch football. I had glowing white Adidas running shoes and wore wristbands like the Golden State Warriors' Rick Barry, so it didn't seem right that they'd always beat me to the finish line in our makeshift running races or would leave me on the ground watching one of them tear off on their way to another touchdown.

My cousin drowned in the Thames—the tire was cut down from the tree, his surviving brothers didn't swim in the river anymore—and like everyone else at the funeral, I shook hands with his dad and brothers and kissed my aunt on the cheek and took my turn slowly walking past the open casket. He was only a year older than me, but in his suit and with his folded hands resting on his stomach and a silent smile on his face, it seemed like more than that, it seemed like he was more mature. I wasn't glad he was dead, but I felt as if I was finally better at something than him. Smarter, because I didn't do stupid things like swim in the filthy Thames; superior, because I was alive and he wasn't. "When a man takes to his bed," Baudelaire wrote, "nearly all his friends have a secret desire to see him die; some to prove that his health is inferior to his own, others in the disinterested hope of being able to study the death agony."

When we're children, funeral homes are like horror movie sets the monsters forgot to visit. Whatever unease one experienced upon entering was significantly dissipated when leaving. Yes, it was hushed quiet, a barely detectable pipe organ over the unseen speakers, and there *were* coffins in every room, all of them surrounded by bundles of flowers and some of them even with their lids open to reveal their closed-eyed occupants. But there was something too bureaucratic, too communal about the whole affair to provide one with authentic chills and thrills. If the service wasn't much more interesting than any other time someone at the front of the room talked and talked and talked while everyone else had to sit still and be quiet and listen, and if you happened to be stuck sitting beside your Aunt Marjorie for the entire hour or more (good for five dollars on your birthday and ten at Christmas, but bowlegged and wheezy and with shiver-inducing halitosis), how could a funeral home be anything other than what it seemed to be: somewhere you had to go to do something that had to be done?

Cemeteries, however, were something else. Bicycling over with a couple of friends on a sunny summer afternoon, the big green trees, big leafy lungs, breathing in and out the warm, billowing breeze, and wherever you rode or walked the wonderfully soothing smell of freshly mowed grass, "It might," as Shelley claimed, "make one in love with death, to think that one should be buried in so sweet a place." But it wasn't only bucolic charm and calm. It sounded quiet and felt slow and looked so empty (but in fact was so full) it encouraged you to shut up and slow down and empty your mind (quite an accomplishment when it comes to ordinarily ceaselessly chattering thirteen-year-old boys). Empty your mind to better take in what was all around you, underneath you, everywhere. A small city of the dead. People, couples, children, families that were alive once, just like you are now, just look: born on this day of this year, died on that day of that year, Rest in Peace, Loved Forever, Will Not Be Forgotten.

And except perhaps for some of the more recent arrivals, with newer headstones not yet defaced with identity-eroding lichen and memorialized with a jar of wildflowers or a weather-battered wreath, all long forgotten.

Like most people, I fulfilled—and then some— Goethe's summation of adolescence's exasperating (if only to others) self-absorption: "In his youth, everybody believes that the world began to exist only when he was born, and that everything really exists only for his sake." It's not so much that you're inconsiderate of other people as it is that it's difficult to believe that they actually exist. Obviously they do, in a way—everywhere you look, there goes another one—but not in the same singular way you do. How could they? If everyone is unique, then no one is. Other planets are out there (just ask the scientists, they have ways of proving it), but they exist only in relation to you—you, the life-conferring sun. We—*me*—is the primal prime mover.

A cemetery is an excellent ego corrective. What I think and what I feel and what I do and what I want and WHO I AM doesn't seem quite so unique and important when everywhere you look (and step) there are thousands of others who must also have at one time considered what they thought and felt and did and wanted and were was also extraordinarily unique and important. Life tends to move too quickly—so many things to think and feel and do and want and be— for one to notice that other people exist. Only in the infrequent instances when we love another individual as Simone Weil defined love ("Belief in the existence of other human beings as such is love") does the solipsistic scrim we've constructed collapse. But in a cemetery it's difficult to deny that life simply doesn't give a shit about us. Actually, that's the extent of life's concern for us once we're dead and have gone on to join all the other busy, self-important people underneath the ground: that we make good fertilizer for the lovely trees and the sweet-smelling grass and all the pretty flowers.

A stroll though a cemetery is the anti-selfie ("Look at me! Look at me!" "Why?" "Because it's *me*!"). The next logical question a graveyard's contemplation inspires in the moderately meditative adolescent goes even further in helping to obliterate our cherished illusion of sanctified selfhood. *How do you take your eternity, Sir, with burial or cremation*? It's like that childhood game of how you'd rather die, except this time it isn't a game and the question isn't hypothetical. Of course, the predicament isn't as grim as laid out here: there's not only the option of being either boxed and buried or burned and scattered (or interred or vased); there also remains the possibility of donating your body to science so that medical students can improve their scalpel work and anatomy knowledge by slicing open your carcass and removing and inspecting your organs. It's not as if they won't return them eventually—all extracted body parts will be stuffed back inside you (not unlike the stuffing that's crammed inside a turkey)—before your corpse is either buried or burned, usually en masse. And here we are confronted with that same unsavoury choice again.

The principal argument for burial over cremation would seem to be that one avoids being cremated. It's difficult to imagine ever being dead enough not to feel the fiery blast of the crematory furnace. And even if frosty logic prevails and one reasons that "I" won't be the corpse being charred—no "I" being in existence any longer to experience any pain (or anything else)—there still remains the image of one's loved ones being slid into the roaring oven and emerging as amorphous embers. We might not be there to feel self-pity at our own blazing transformation and ashy end, but how can we avoid horror and sorrow when our family and friends are one moment cherished intimates and the next moment flaming, bubbling flesh? At least when a coffin is resting underneath the earth we know that a relatively intact facsimile of our parent or spouse or child rests there, and not some powdery proxy. This is why people are often buried in their favourite clothes or along with a cherished or emblematic object or with photographs of their surviving loved ones: we're saying goodbye to all that they once were. We're saying goodbye to *them*. They might be sealed up inside a $6,000 bucket and there might be formaldehyde in their veins and an autopsy scar might run the length of their chests, but *they're* in there. Admittedly, it's not much comfort, but it's some. And at times like these, some is something.

But then there are the worms. Those busy, busy worms and insects and other subterranean trespassers that are as patient as they are persistent. It might take several generations of maggoty discipline and steady burrowing, but the worms always win. A Sterling Deluxe Stainless Steel Casket with an immaculate white silk interior or not, mother's kind face will eventually be a mouldy meal for the first arrivals to make it through the casket to what's left of the meat and bones. Cremation at least cheats the worms. And if life really is ashes to ashes, dust to dust, why not bypass middleman Time and get on with the job at hand as soon as possible? Whether scattered across the water or launched into the wind, merging with the universe sure as hell beats waiting around to become creepy-crawler feces.

So what's the final tally? Who wins how we should ideally end up? As in life, so in death, there is no clear winner. Burial or cremation would seem to equal six of one, a half dozen of the other. Perhaps the only correct answer is akin to the one the ailing elderly sometimes give when asked how they're feeling: *Take my advice*, they'll say. *Don't get old.* We laugh, we almost understand, we nod in sympathy. But people grow old. And people die. And here we are back where we started.

But maybe the question goes deeper than what inevitably degraded form we wish to end up as. Perhaps it's really about how important it is to the individual to concretize (sometimes literally) their desire to be remembered. Like the church benefactor whose generous philanthropy is sometimes subconsciously connected to the desire to get a better seat at the foot of God when his or her time to celestially ascend arrives, the purchaser of the biggest, most expensive, most ostentatious tombstone or mausoleum in the cemetery believes they're buying remembrance. Someone who has a grave that large and/or expensive must have been someone special, a fact that future generations simply won't be able to overlook or forget. When it comes to immortality, size matters.

Except, of course, it doesn't. Nothing does. You don't need the wise preacher of the Old Testament to tell you that all is vanity and that nothing and no one is remembered for very long. Toppled, broken gravestones scrubbed all-but-blank by decades of season after indifferent season are lesson enough. More than illustrating the futility of the human longing for immortality, an old cemetery reminds us of human beings' colossal arrogance. "The smaller the mind, the greater the conceit," wrote Aesop. The bigger the tomb, the larger the delusion.

So what's to be done? To leave instructions for our remains to be scattered and thereby escape the sin of a shamefully prideful monument to selfhood predicated upon egoistic illusions of immortality? Good for you and whoopdefuckingdo. Ashes in the sea or bones at the bottom of a hole, we're all poor Yoricks, of whom those who do manage to remember us for a little while might well ask, "Where be your gibes now? Your gambols? Your songs? Your flashes of merriment that were wont to set the table on a roar?"

Silence. End scene.

Psychologically, epistemologically, existentially—all the signs testify to how difficult (if not impossible) it is to wholly comprehend one's own eventual non-existence. Even the most contemplative of us ends up tripping over our intractable ego on the way to full comprehension. When it comes to grasping the truth of our own annihilation, Ivan Ilych's dilemma is uncomfortably familiar: "The syllogism he had learnt from Kiesewetter's logic: 'Caius is a man, men are mortal, therefore Caius is mortal,' had always seemed to him correct as applied to Caius, but certainly not as applied to himself." The most logical logic simply isn't—can't be—logical.

There's no such roadblock to understanding when it comes to the death of someone close to us, however. Particularly someone we love. Here, to say that a great deal of imagination isn't necessary to grasp death's devastating reality is to commit a cruelly absurd understatement. Our death might always remain a mystery to ourselves, but our wife's or husband's or partner's couldn't be more obvious. It means pain. Mental, emotional, physical pain. It means sorrow. For their loss of their life, for our loss of them in ours, for a world that can never be the same. It means anger. At them for dying, at life for taking them, at us for being useless to do anything about it. It means stunned insensibility and piercing rage and every unpredictable, exhausting variation in between.

Novelists need to be good fabricators. Life, no matter how rich and interesting to the individual, is rarely compelling enough for the purposes of the novelist. You make things up so that your book makes more sense. I wanted the central protagonist of my novel *I Was There the Night He Died* to be a man standing at life's ground zero, all of the comforting certainties that had once been so sustaining—work, love, family, chemical self-medication—having collapsed around him. I pulled from my own life certain experiences with loss and lost direction, but the fundamental damage done to Sam Samson was the death of his wife, Sara, in an automobile accident. Thankfully, my wife is still alive, but I remembered a story a high-school friend told me many years previous when I bumped into him while home visiting my parents. I'd heard that his young wife had been killed a year or so before in a single car collision, and when we had a chance to talk at the bar where we ran into each other, two things stuck with me—stuck with me for more than twenty years, when I came to write my novel.

He told me he said goodbye to his wife at 8:30 in the morning before they both set off for work, and that he was making arrangements for her gravestone by five p.m. that same day. One more chilling lesson in the terrifying capriciousness of everyday existence: everything in its place and everything acting as it should until you're suddenly selecting the slab of marble that's going to sit on your wife's head for eternity. "We plan, God laughs," goes the Yiddish proverb. With Gods like these, who needs the devil?

He also told me that when he returned to their empty home after the funeral, his first impulse was to tell her about it. Part of this is obviously habit—wanting to know what time it is, we instinctively look for the clock hanging over the kitchen table although we were the one who moved it to the other side of the room last week—but part of it is because there was a reason this was the person we lived with and chose to spend our life with and trusted beyond all others. "Love does not consist in gazing at each other but in looking together in the same direction," wrote Saint-Exupery. Talking to someone who isn't alive anymore isn't nearly as odd as not continuing to need someone to rely on and confide in and who sees the world the same way we do.

A parent's death has its own distinctive fatal flavour. Mothers and fathers are rarely our principal confidants (and if they are, they've probably done an inferior job of out-of-the-nest-and-off-you-go parenting). As we age, however, hopefully we come to better understand and appreciate them as individuals with their own personalities and pasts, dreams and disappointments, but they'll always be our Mom and Dad and will always be unconditionally there—there for *us*—as undeviating in their benevolent ubiquity as anything (and certainly anyone) can be. Until they're not. Until they die. First one, then the other, then we're grown-up orphans. It doesn't matter that, if we're lucky, by the time they're old, we're adults with independent lives and perhaps children of our own and are even able to occasionally reverse the parent-child roles and now be the stronger, more worldly-wise, more supportive ones. Not until your parents are dead do you really grow up. Grown up to understand how alone we all really are. No tart aphorism from a French existentialist on the cold, uncaring solitariness of existence can have the impact of one's parents being gone. Forever. And this time, Mommy and Daddy won't make it right. Would if they could. But they can't.

A parent outliving a child is an entirely different sort of grief, something most of us, mercifully, will never understand. When an elderly parent dies after a long, (hopefully) full life, there's sadness, naturally, and even incredulity that the loved one is gone forever, but there's also a sense of "fairness," an acknowledgment that the life cycle has been completed, as well as, quite often, relief (for both the sufferer and for those who had to witness his or her suffering). But if on some basic level any death can't help but seem "wrong," the loss of a child can only feel obscene. Talk to a parent who's suffered a son or a daughter's death— even years later—and the strain to convey even a portion of their sorrow is agonizing to witness, incommunicability the most eloquent expression of their anguish possible. It's probably not a coincidence that the two couples I know who suffered the death of a child each ended up divorced. It's possible that they might have split up eventually, but both of the husbands admitted that their partner's presence couldn't help but be a daily, corporeal reminder of their child's death and a shameful, if undeniable, element in the breakup. No one was responsible, it was never a matter of blame, but a new partner, a new home, a new life made them hurt just a little bit less. And with suffering this great, a little can feel like a lot.

Sorrow as a consequence of all manner of familial loss is ordinarily a foregone conclusion. But an argument could be made that the love one feels for a friend, a real friend ("One of [whose] most beautiful qualities," Seneca wrote in his *Letters from a Stoic*, "is to understand and be understood") is in some ways superior to familial love. Our parents *have* to love us (as we, though perhaps not to the same degree, must love them), just as we are compelled to love our own children. Biology-based, nature-necessitated unconditional love is just that: unconditional. But a friend is a choice ("The soul selects her own society," Emily Dickinson wrote). A choice made against great odds. Whether good, bad, or (as is most often the case) a maddening mix of both, we all have families. But to find one genuine friend—to discover one person we choose to align ourselves with for life—in a world crowded with what often seems only workmates, neighbours, casual acquaintances, professional contacts, and people to whom we would prefer to remain strangers, is a rare triumph. And to be deeply mourned when death decides that the friendship is over.

As difficult as it would have been to believe at the time, the first friend of mine who died, died young (I was the same age—thirty—when it happened, which seemed, if not ancient, at least bordering on incipient middle-age). Our relationship had always been aggressively ambivalent: a very real, very deep connection based on a mutual love of the right writers and righteous musicians and a shared belief in how serious having fun is and how much fun being serious can be, equalled by an intense competitiveness born of an insecurity that said that two people coming from the same small town couldn't both possibly go on to create fulfilling lives in the big city based on a love of beautiful sentences, high harmonies, and high ideals. ("It is not enough to succeed," Wilfred Sheed wrote, paraphrasing La Rochefoucauld; "a friend must also fail.") One minute you were relieved and emboldened to be looking at someone who truly understood, who really *got it*, and the next minute, there was that guy who thought he was some kind of big deal, that pretentious little shit from Chatham, Ontario, who thought he was better than everybody else. I don't have a biological brother, but this was what I imagined having one was like: a lot of laughing, a lot of yelling, and a lot of affection and aggravation so tightly tied up together it was hard to tell sometimes which was which.

When he died—when he died by suicide—we'd had no contact for three years. It wasn't any one incident or argument that led to the freeze; we'd both independently come to the same conclusion: there simply wasn't enough oxygen in the room if we both wanted to breathe as deeply and freely as we needed to. He'd long since moved to Montreal, and I was living in Texas when I got the phone call from a mutual friend saying he'd died. I was shocked, of course, but can't claim to have been unduly despondent. Three years without the exchange of a single spoken or written word when you're young seems like centuries, and I was knee-deep in the muck of my own life, struggling, like most people approaching or just past thirty, to discover the mud-obscured path I was supposed to be travelling. I talked to my wife (who I met through him) about it, I sent the family a condolence card, I

got back to work on my novel. If anything, I was bothered I wasn't more bothered.

I needn't have worried—life rarely lets you off that
easy. More than two decades later, I still have the same
basic dream (although much less frequently now, only
a couple of times a year). He's there, I'm there, and I'm
surprised to find he's alive. I either ask him why people
think he's dead or how it's possible for him to be
deceased yet right here standing in front of me. He
never answers. I also usually pay him some kind of
oblique compliment (noting the quality of his home
library or record collection is a common one). Not
enough to make either of us uncomfortable, but enough
that he knows I respect him, something, I realize now,
I never did—or did enough—when he was alive. For a
long time I wondered why, now that I had the chance,
I never asked him anything about the fact that he'd
taken his own life. Twenty years and many more deaths
(including a couple other suicides) later, I don't wonder anymore. "Whatever can happen at any time can
happen today," Seneca wrote. The mystery isn't any
longer how this or that death happened or why, but
that we were ever lucky enough to be alive at all.

Death tends to be most common as a topic of conversation and food for reflection when we're young, old,

or ailing. Although death is usually far removed from childhood or adolescent experience, for that reason alone it's easier to talk about. Also, because it's, if not forbidden, at least discouraged as a topic of conversation (like sex), it's even fun, feels slightly scandalous, to discuss it. Who didn't toy around with the "Would you rather be shot or stabbed?" question, the "If it had to be one or the other, would you rather drown or suffocate" game?

The desire to be scared in the form of watching horror movies is another one of youth's ways of flirting with the enticingly unfathomable. In my case, "watch" isn't the appropriate verb—"gorge" would be more apposite. Not just because it's more accurate, but because it better captures the tang of my cinematic gluttony. I couldn't get enough of vampires who bit, mummies who choked, werewolves who clawed and tore, prehistoric monsters risen from their frozen tombs by hydrogen bombs (and man's nefarious hubris) and driven to stomp, smash, and skewer. Granted, the thrill of the fright was often diluted by the implausibility of the plots or the wooden acting or the dead (and not in a good way) dialogue—or, frequently, all three—but underneath all of the amateurishness there was still the tingle of good old terror. In retrospect, this more than occasional improbability likely aided in maximizing the films' fright factor. If I hadn't been intermittently reminded that the werewolf looked more like a college football team's overly furry, frowning mascot than a half-man, half-wolf killing machine or been made suspicious of those flying saucers that resembled the tinfoil pie plates my mother used for her baking, I might not have been able to stay plunked in front of the television until movie's end. A little bit of laughter—especially derisive laughter—help makes the terror go down.

With films that featured ghosts, exorcisms, or the occult, however, things could be more complicated. There was still a fair share of cinematic clunkers, spirits that went boo-boo instead of *Boo!* in the night, but there were also movies like *The Changeling*, *The Exorcist*, and *The Haunting*, films where the production values were high, the acting was professional, and, most importantly, the writing was generally first-rate. Because the movies seemed real, so did the terror. In addition, the fright value of a satanically possessed child or a haunted house wasn't generated by "look-out-behind-you!" suspense or blood-and-guts shock and gore, but by things, for the most part, unseen. Unseen and therefore impossible to unequivocally deny. Dracula and zombies and pissed-off mummies were the paranormal price one paid for a ticket on a day-trip aboard the supernatural express, with stops along the way at Death, Decay, and Dread, but no one believed in vampires and the resurrected recently deceased. Not really. But demons and lost souls…

Aside from absorbing the usual amount of Christian conditioning that goes with growing up in North American society, religion-wise, I was raised working-class, small-town Canada circa the 1970s: God means Love and be nice to other people and they'll (probably) be nice to you and beware of all those spouting Holy Joe hocus-pocus. For the most part, I was a contented believer in non-belief. But one couldn't really know for sure, could one? Not 100%. Just because we don't see something—particularly something chill-inducing—doesn't mean it's not real. Maybe—just maybe—the fear generated by a dark room at the top of the stairs, a strange sound in the middle of the night, a well-told ghost story that someone claimed actually happened, was rooted in a strange, inexplicable, but nonetheless bona fide reality. *Hamlet* wasn't on my reading list until Mr. Rose's grade thirteen English class, but "There are more things in Heaven and Earth, Horatio, than are dreamt of in your philosophy" could have appeared on the television screen prior to the start of every Saturday night horror film and I would have nodded away in at least partial understanding.

Later on, as one gradually grows more cognizant of death and the genuinely frightening, as opposed to cinematically fabricated, consequences of mortality (that's it, that's all, there ain't any more), there's even an appealing logic to the likely illogicality of ghosts and demons and three-day exorcisms. On the one hand, a gleefully sadistic, projectile-vomiting, profanity-spewing possessed person can ruin your entire day (my parents saw *The Exorcist* when it was released over forty years ago and remember one viewer throwing up and two couples fleeing the theatre out of fright or disgust). On the other hand, if the devil exists, *ergo*, God (however defined) does too. If there's evil on the other side, that means there *is* another side. Monsters make metaphysics possible. Because there's something even more terrifying than heads spinning around on their owners' necks and houses that want you to vacate them strongly enough that blood flows from the shower faucet and the walls whisper your name: nothingness. Confronted with death's promise of never-ending nothing, the devil can be a comforting thought.

At the other end of the age spectrum, the British man of letters John Cowper Powys believed that old age wasn't only a predicament to be endured, it was also the provider of a potential attitudinal advantage, something he wrote about in *The Art of Growing Old*:

The one supreme advantage that Old Age possesses over Middle Age and Youth is its nearness to Death. The very thing that makes it seem pitiable to those less threatened and therefore less enlightened ages of man is the thing that deepens, heightens, and thickens out its felicity...[This is because] we poor dullards of habit and custom, we besotted and befuddled takers of life for granted, require the hell of a flaming thunderbolt to rouse us to the fact that every single second of conscious life is a miracle past reckoning, a marvel past all computation.

Utilizing a flaming thunderbolt for an alarm clock isn't the nicest way to wake up, but it does tend to ensure that you don't sleep through what's important. Such as your life.

That said, reflecting upon death in our advanced years isn't always as amusing or enriching as it was when we were young—not when one goes to bed at night wondering whether or not one will wake up in the morning. For the elderly, it's only natural to ponder mortality in a resolutely pragmatic fashion—particularly one's own. My eighty-two-year-old father-in-law admitted to my wife that every time he's light-headed or has a bad case of indigestion or a sudden headache, part of him can't help thinking: *Is this it? Is this the stroke or heart attack or aneurism that kills me?* My seventy-six-year-old father told me recently that after he'd been reminded that my wife and I had returned to Canada from the United States and grad school twenty years ago, he thought two things: first, that it seemed like only yesterday, and two, that he very likely wouldn't be around the next time another two decades flew past. I said what I was supposed to say—*Hey, none of us is guaranteed to be here for another twenty minutes, let alone another twenty years; It's not how long you live, it's how well; Who knows? Some people do, after all, live into their late-nineties and lead happy, productive lives*—but I'm sure it made little or no impact. Everyone knows the clock is ticking, but the near-octogenarian can hear it *tick tick tick* a little more loudly than most.

Gore Vidal told the story of visiting the home of Elizabeth Bowen and, while accompanying the much older writer on a wet and windy, leaf-falling-and-flying autumn walk, remarking that fall was his favourite season. Bowen replied that it used to be hers, too, when she was young, but he would discover that when he was her age, spring becomes the most anticipated time of the year. Out of deference to the senior writer Vidal said nothing, only inwardly noted the uncharacteristic conventionality, not to mention feebleness, of her belief. Until he turned senior citizen and was surprised to learn he'd come to believe the same thing himself. The brisk, bracing winds and refreshing chill of October is youth's seasonal soundtrack—things to get done yesterday and an icy flame of industry lit underneath one's ass today. But once one is old enough to imagine the very different chill of the tomb as something more than horror-film theoretical, May's reviving warmth and nurturing showers and gentle breezes are what the aging body and spirit really crave. When the graveyard moves in next door, whistling won't distract you for long from the spectre of your new neighbour. The elderly are often too busy, both physically and psychologically, to spend much time voluntarily contemplating death. It is fragile, flickering life that needs one's assistance in remaining existent.

Then there are those who, elderly or not, are (or are afraid they might be) mortally ill. A writer friend who is battling lung cancer as I write this book has approached her illness as she has every other challenge in her life: with dogged, methodical, intelligent effort. When I asked her if, because of her disease, she felt as if she'd gained any unique insights into mortality, she was quick to answer that, while of course she couldn't avoid occasionally thinking about death and all that she was determined not to lose (particularly if she was having a bad day or suffering a long night), it was life she was focused on. Whether this meant diligently following her various doctors' orders or independently investigating alternative healing methods or simply maintaining a positive attitude (including asking her friends to send positive thoughts her way), the act of living was what consumed her most, not the thought of dying. She mentioned a terminally ill man who was in the same ward as her when she was first admitted into hospital and before she was definitively diagnosed, how the man kept the small reading light attached to his headboard blazing all night long regardless of whether or not he was awake. She said that at first it bothered her—not because it kept her from sleeping, but because it just seemed wasteful and, well, wrong. After she was told what she hadn't wanted to hear—that she had lung cancer and faced a long, difficult road to (hopefully) recovery—she said the light never upset her again. Found it sort of comforting, in fact.

Contemporary medicine and its murky morality also contribute toward making it difficult to pay death's mystery its due when one is seriously ill or injured. Don't misunderstand: in the process of passing a kidney stone several years ago, the hospital didn't own enough morphine to satiate me. Being in touch with my feelings about pain or contemplating the relationship between physical suffering and mental forbearance wasn't a priority. What I wanted was the pain to stop and the drugs that could make that happen. As many drugs and in as great a quantity as possible (and certainly more than the nurses were willing to give me). When I did finally begin to feel—not normal: my brain too cozily comforted for that, my body and its angry agenda pleasantly floating far, far away—discomfort-free, *then* I could begin to think about something other than how to stop hurting. Comfort first, then philosophy.

Powerful painkillers aren't the only way that the medical profession eases our path to oblivion. Sometimes terminally ill patients don't know that they're going to die—and sooner than later—because their doctors and/or family and friends don't tell them. Not unequivocally, anyway. (*It doesn't look good, but miracles do happen...*) On the one hand, this seems tantamount to the worst sort of institutional oppression: it's the patient's life—and death—and yet he or she is sometimes the one with the least knowledge of their critical condition. It's hard to make peace with death when one is still fully invested in the fight for life.

On the other hand, some people, on some very primal, self-preservatory level, simply don't *want* to know, and tacitly cooperate with this organizational obfuscation or even encourage it. Wanting to keep his mind as clear and sharp as possible, for as long as possible, so as to better fight the most important battle of his life, another cancer-stricken friend of mine eschewed the most powerful of opiates until almost the final hours of his life, and was raving the day of his death. Not incoherent raving, but I DONT WANT TO DIE raving, I'M NOT READY TO DIE raving, THIS ISN'T FUCKING FAIR raving. It's difficult to believe that he benefitted much from his commitment to relative clear-headedness. The dying have got enough to think about just trying to stay alive and maximizing what happiness they're capable of in what little time they have left. Death—its comprehensive contemplation, anyway—is for the living.

Here's another irony, then, to add to life's already considerable inventory: the most opportune time to think about death isn't when we're young or when we're old or sick, but when we're happily, healthily immersed in life. And not because of metaphysical masochism or a sense of dutiful humanism, but because, as Montaigne noted, "He who would teach men to die would teach them to live." Not that we can ever simply read a book or listen to a podcast and—eureka!—instant enlightenment. The deepest, most lasting learning is done primarily by our searching self. "Let us only listen," Montaigne advised. "We tell ourselves all we most need." And if we can better educate ourselves about what death is, we'll certainly know more of what life consists. Pondering death isn't morbid or frivolous. Not unless we believe that asking what makes for a fully realized life is as well. To become better acquainted with death is to better comprehend life. And without understanding, there can never be true happiness, only, at best, intermittent pleasure. "Know thyself," the ancient Greeks famously advised. Which also means knowing what that same self will not be some day—alive.

PART TWO

PART TWO

When the psychiatrist Elizabeth Kubler-Ross published her pioneering *On Death and Dying* in 1969, she intended that her now famous "five stages of grief" (i. Denial and Isolation; ii. Anger; iii. Bargaining; iv. Depression; v. Acceptance) be applied to the individual's psychological journey toward personal extinction. *On Death and Dying* was the result of Kubler-Ross' work with terminally ill patients at the University of Chicago medical school and was inspired by what she felt was a dearth of curriculum in medical schools on the taboo subject of death and dying. Kubler-Ross believed that, although there were exceptions (stages skipped, stages never achieved), human beings when confronted with their own mortality tend to move through a series of identifiable steps on the way to eventual acceptance of their impending death. In spite of undergoing the sort of periodic criticism that comes with being a half-century old, groundbreaking theory (e.g. that environment—either positive or negative—plays a determining factor in the individual's experience), Kubler-Ross' five stages have held up well as the best paradigm for what death does to our emotions and intellect before finishing with our bodies.

When it comes to most of the elemental and most interesting stuff, Whitman had it right: "And what I assume you shall assume, / For every atom belonging to me as good belongs to you." Letting the part stand for the whole, Kubler-Ross' theory can just as easily and profitably be applied to human beings as a species. Different skin colours and different languages; different geographies and different customs; different sexual orientations and different political inclinations: nevertheless, we are all born, we all suffer, we all die, with only the suffering part varying from one individual to the next (those from country X, from war or starvation; those from country Y, from ennui or too much fried fatty food). And the first thing that the majority of human beings tend to do when entertaining the thought of death is to reject the question. Death? Mine? Me? What death? This is Kubler-Ross' first stage.

(i)

Anthropologists like Sir Edward Burnett Tylor and Sir James George Frazer have provided convincing evidence that the belief in personal immortality permeated the earliest human societies. Among the first there was the conviction that brave warriors were rewarded for their heroism in battle by going to a place of everlasting happiness after their gallant deaths. Later, the idea that personal immortality was attainable for all became widespread and was often tied to ethical conduct. The ancient Egyptians held that, among other things, piety to the gods would assure a happy afterlife. Most Christians and Muslims ascribe to the same basic quid pro quo theology: you do something nice for God (worship Him alone and follow His precepts), He'll do something nice for you (grant you everlasting life). If you ask people today what religion means, most will mention the importance of following rules laid down a couple or more millennia ago (because otherwise life would be banal and bewildering) and the existence of something resembling the Christian idea of heaven (because otherwise life would be meaningless).

One day in grade five during the first period after lunch, our class, along with all of the other grade five classes at school, was marched to the gymnasium single file, no talking, please, and no horsing around in the hall. Usually this meant a school assembly or watching an educational film or, if it was close to Christmas, singing carols. On this particular afternoon we were going to listen to the Gideons. *Who are the Gideons?* someone asked. *You'll find out soon enough*, Mrs. Newbury answered. *And I hope you'll give them the same undivided attention you give to me.* All I needed to know was that we wouldn't be having math class. Who needed to know anything more than that? Even if you never won any awards, like me (unless you counted an attendance badge, which no one did, since it had more to do with your Mom never letting you stay home from school than anything you did) or the film was lame (like the story of the fur trade) or the carols were lamer than lame (Rudolph the Red Nosed Reindeer? Give me a break. We weren't *babies*), the announcement that there was going to be a trip to the auditorium was always welcome news.

The Gideons turned out to be a man and a woman who looked like our teachers, but who never stopped smiling and who talked about God, although not for very long and only in the context of what they were doing at our school: distributing free copies of the New Testament. After they passed out the little red books to all of the Grade Fives sitting cross-legged on the gym floor, they made everyone write their full name and that day's date in the space provided on the inside front cover. We didn't discuss God at home and my parents and I never went to church, but the man and the woman made it seem like a big deal that we were all finally ready to have our own Bible, like it was a real grown-up thing. Plus, it was free. It wasn't every day that you got something 100% free.

If the Gideons had been hoping for instant conversion and fervent faith in return for their gift, they would have been disappointed. I didn't begin to nag my parents to take me to church or start to think about God all of the time or even read my complimentary copy of the New Testament (it stayed in the drawer of my bedside table, where I also kept my hockey card doubles and the wristwatch I never wore because you had to wind it all the time). But I knew it was there, and a few years later I began to pray before I went to bed. We'd always recited the Lord's Prayer at school after singing the national anthem and before the morning announcements crackled over the PA, but on my own and on my knees and one-on-one with the Big Guy in the Sky was something new. *Now I lay me down to sleep / I pray the Lord my soul to keep. / And if I die before I wake / I pray the Lord my soul to take.* God (Jesus? The distinction wasn't clear) suitably invoked, I would ask the Lord to please look after me, my Mom and my Dad, and our cat (and in that order). It wasn't about what I felt either before I prayed or during, but what occurred afterward. In bed under the blankets with the lights off, I felt as if I'd done my duty, that I'd covered all of my bases, that I'd bought a little piece of spiritual life insurance for my family and me. If I forgot to do it or was just too lazy or too cold to get out of bed, it didn't feel as if I was letting God down, but more like I was potentially endangering the Godly goodwill I'd built up. One thing I knew about God was that He wouldn't put up with disrespect. I'd climb from underneath the covers and get down on my knees and close my eyes and say what I had to say. Then I felt like I could go to sleep.

The only time I talked to God when I wasn't in my pajamas was that same year at Christmas. December twenty-fifth had always been toys under the tree and too much food in everybody's stomach and that was all right with me. What was Joy to the World all about if not lots of getting and plenty of overeating? But something was different that Christmas. Part of it was probably my age—the beginning of the tetchy teenage years, everyone a fool and everything just too stupid for words—but I think my nightly prayers had something to do with it as well. Becoming too old for toys, the stuff lust of Christmases past had begun to wane, the glut of wrapped-and-bowed and ready-to-be-ripped-open gifts gathered under the plastic pine tree in the living room not so much tantalizing anymore as embarrassingly obvious and unnecessary (sweaters Dad wouldn't wear more than once or twice, jewellery from the mall Mom would inevitably say was beautiful before it disappeared forever inside her jewellery box). Sitting at the dinner table for the annual Christmas gorge fest, I found myself irritated that my father was wearing grey track pants. We were never a family to stand on ceremony (good jeans—i.e. no holes—and clean running shoes sufficient for when visiting relatives, and none of that "May I please speak to so-and-so?" telephone etiquette stuff when a simple "Is Eddie there?" would do)—but even for us this seemed a little much. Or, rather, a little too little. Maybe I hadn't read the Bible, but I knew what today was: Jesus' birthday. They didn't shut all of the stores and bump all of the regular shows off TV for Christmas specials and movies for nothing.

As soon as I'd finished my apple pie and ice cream I put on my coat and hat and said I was going outside. It wasn't even nine o'clock yet, but already the night was as dark as it was going to get. The sky was smeared with stars, but the streetlights were brighter, so I walked until our subdivision stopped and the cornfield began. There wasn't any question of calling on anyone—it was Christmas and nighttime, everyone would be with their families—so I sat on the frozen ground at the edge of the farmer's field and looked at the stars. Some people knew what the Milky Way was and where to find the Big Dipper, but all I could see were stars. I sang "Away in a Manger"—softly, to myself—and I didn't cry, but I knew I would if I kept singing because I could feel the warmth of the tears welling in my eyes in contrast to my cold face. It was sad about the little baby Jesus and there being no room anywhere for a crib, but even without words the song would have been sad. Certain kinds of music were like that.

"Jesus," I said, even more quietly. "It's your birthday." I wasn't technically praying because my eyes weren't closed and I wasn't on my knees and my hands in their gloves hung at my sides, but it felt like the first time that I wasn't just perfunctorily paying the dues on my deity insurance. "People don't know. People, they just don't understand." Even then, as I said it, I knew I didn't really understand either—didn't even know what I meant when I said people didn't understand—but it was sincere incomprehension. "Happy birthday, Jesus," I said. I looked at the stars some more, until the tip of my nose began to burn with cold, and started back home. I wondered if my Mom would let me have another piece of pie and some more ice cream.

Jesus departed just as suddenly as He'd arrived. The next year was high school, and there were adolescent ethical realms that demanded to be deciphered and respected if one didn't want to get left behind and be, you know, a loser, as well as gleaming new numinous ideas and ideals to wonder at and worship. Knowing that Thou Shalt Not Talk to Dweebs and making sure to never take the name *Chatham Collegiate Institute Cougars* in vain weren't the kind of commandments written down on any tablet, and aching to get a girl, any girl, to go to second base as well as wanting to make the Junior Football Team as badly as you ever wanted to do all the right things in order to win a free pass to heaven might have been a drop-off in degrees of spiritual ambition, but they kept me busy. Religion is religion; we get our gods where we can. And the Gideon's little red book didn't stand a chance alongside girls whose bra straps showed through their thin cotton T-shirts and visions of returning an interception for a last-minute, game-winning touchdown.

Of course, there was still that whole dying and being dead for eternity thing. Theoretically, anyway. Every teenager secretly knows that they'll live forever, or at least long enough to do and be absolutely anything they want. Immortality is easy to imagine—is nearly impossible *not* to imagine—when your body is a machine that grows stronger and quicker every day and there are an infinity of places you've never been and people you've never met and experiences you've never had. There's not enough time in the day for finitude. But dreams don't last forever, and neither does immortality—usually begins to wind down around the same time as your initial soul-sapping, minimum-wage job, the first time Cupid punches you *thump* in the heart, the first time someone you were going to know forever unexpectedly becomes a stranger. If your boss at Burger King can steal your time; if your grade nine girlfriend can own your soul; if your best friend forever, no matter what, no joking, for real, can turn out to be just another jerk: maybe, just maybe, you're not invincible. And maybe, just maybe, the world can get along just fine without you.

On the other hand, some people never trade in their Bible for a chance at football heroism and the quest to get their clammy hand underneath someone else's sweater. And for them, the promise of eternal life is often foremost among their chosen religion's many allures. "In our sad condition," Martin Luther wrote, "our only consolation is the expectancy of another life. Here below all is incomprehensible." Most deniers of death's ultimate preeminence aren't quite as sanguine as was the nineteenth-century American novelist Catherine Maria Sedgwick, who, comparing heaven with her hometown of Stockbridge, Massachusetts, declared, "I expect no very violent transition," but the hope is essentially the same: somehow, in some form, I'll still be me. Forever. From Alexander Pope's "The Dying Christian to his Soul":

> I mount! I fly!
> O grave! where is thy victory?
> O death! Where is thy sting?

Endless tomes and entire lifetimes have been dedicated to the question of God's existence or non-existence, so no simple thumbs up or thumbs down here would contribute much to the conversation (because that's what this is—a conversation—a never-ending, existentially enriching dialogue with oneself that only finishes when you do). It is worth noting, however, that not every theist simultaneously posits a personal God or the concept of personal immortality. Voltaire, for instance, believed in an existence-begetting God, yet also thought that the idea of a Supreme Being who took an interest in human affairs and granted human beings eternal life was the result of a combination of intellectual and emotional frailty and simple vanity. "Nobody thinks of giving an immortal soul to a flea," he remarked. For him, "God gave us the gift of life; it is up to us to give ourselves the gift of living well."

The basis of not only most of Western philosophy but also the theoretical underpinning of Christianity originates in the work of Plato and Aristotle. Plato's strict division between body and soul as well as his theory of forms, in which the physical world is an imitation of a perfect, unchanging reality, are the philosophical prototypes of two key elements of Christian theology. St. Augustine, for example, so influential in helping to mold much of what we now understand as Christian theoretical dogma, was profoundly influenced by Plato via the work of Plotinus and other third-century neo-Platonists. Aristotle's contribution to Christian theology is also profound, his work influencing both Anselm (via his principles of Being as outlined in *Metaphysics* and *Physics*) and Thomas Aquinas (who referred to Aristotle as simply "The Philosopher"), who utilized Aristotle's concept of the prime mover as the basis for his own cosmological argument for God's existence.

And yet, while Plato confidently held that the soul is immortal (in the *Phaedo*, he offers four separate arguments of varying levels of convincingness for this belief), Aristotle maintained that the soul ceases to exist when the body does. Samuel Taylor Coleridge famously stated that "everybody is born either a Platonist or an Aristotelian," and even if we necessarily file the "Plato vs. Aristotle on Immortality" debate under *Another Place, Another Time*, the question isn't insipidly academic, like "Does that table really exist?" or "Why is there something rather than nothing?" Our attitude toward death matters. It affects the way we live. To a great degree, it *determines* how we live. Intellectual ambivalence is *not* a judicious option. Whether or not the table really exists isn't a priority as long as it manages to support my bottle of wine and bowl of peanuts; whether to spend my time on earth as if I'll somehow exist forever in celestial bliss or only live out my four-score-and-a-bit before becoming worm food, is. And if a tie always goes to the runner, the big question still remains: Who's on first? On second? On third? If logic leaves us seemingly deadlocked, in other words, perhaps it's best to leave logic alone, at least for the time being.

Maybe we should believe because we *need* to believe. William James makes this very case, even if he disguises it as an answer arrived at because of an alternative theory of truth (Pragmatism). In his essay "The Will to Believe" James rejects the agnostic's imperative to withhold belief (or disbelief) because the evidence is not sufficient since "there are...cases where a fact cannot come at all unless a preliminary faith exists in its coming." (Like religious belief, for example, where "evidence might be forever withheld from us unless we met the hypothesis half-way.") What this means for one's belief in personal immortality—and one's preliminary life on earth—if one does decide to play ball with one's desire for, among other things, eternal life, is clear:

> ...the best things are the eternal things, the overlapping things, the things in the universe that throw the last stone, so to speak, and say the final word [and] we are better off even now if we believe [in these eternal things]. The more perfect and more eternal aspect of the universe is represented in our religions as having personal form. The universe is no longer a mere It to us, but a Thou.

If we make the decision to believe, in other words, belief might be more believable. And if we do, and it is, chances are we'll live a happier, more fulfilled life knowing that the universe is not a cold, indifferent place and that existence doesn't end with our corporeal demise.

Of all the criticisms that can be made against this sort of utilitarian understanding of truth, perhaps the simplest, as well as the most deleterious, is that it carries the ignoble whiff of philosophical pleading. Miguel

Unamuno, certainly no atheistic materialist, underlines this tendency in his *The Tragic Sense of Life*, where he asserts that "philosophy is wont, in fact, not infrequently to convert itself into a kind of spiritual pimping. And sometimes into an opiate for lulling sorrows to sleep." Similarly, Nietzsche, while acknowledging that "[i]t is true, there could be a metaphysical world; the absolute possibility of it is hardly to be disputed. We behold all things through the human head and cannot cut off this head," nonetheless, elsewhere, defines faith as "not wanting to know what is true." The "truth" might be multi-faceted; it could prove impossible for human beings to ever entirely comprehend; it's very likely that we tend to fashion it in part (consciously or unconsciously) to suit our own wants and needs. Yep, yep, yep. Whatever it is, though, truth isn't magic. It's not mere wish-fulfillment. If it was, I'd still have hair on my head, the Beatles would never have broken up, and I could be sure to one day be reunited with all of my dearly missed dead dogs. Unfortunately for me, the best way for me to see Barney and Henry again is to close my eyes and try to remember.

Those not so philosophically inclined (i.e. the majority of humanity) tend not to concern themselves with the validity of the various arguments for and against immortality. Most people want to believe, so they believe, rarely bothering to ponder why they're right and why the other side is wrong. Dostoevsky, that most philosophical of novelists, was also, in the best sense of the word, a most ordinary man, whose non-artistic ambitions were simple: to be a happy, healthy, normal human being. (That he failed miserably on all three accounts is beside the point.) "If you were to destroy the belief in immortality in mankind," he claimed, "not only love but every living force on which the continuation of all life in the world depended, would dry up at once." Dostoevsky's unapologetic explanation of why the belief in immortality *should* exist is refreshingly bereft of any hint of the itchy urge for argumentation. This is simply why it *ought* to be, he says. The Italian poet, novelist, and translator Cesare Pavese might have been an atheist, but when he wrote that "Religion consists in believing that everything which happens is extraordinarily important. It can never disappear from the world, for precisely this reason," his reasoning would have appealed to the Russian Orthodox Christian Dostoevsky. This, both men appear to be saying, is simply part of what human beings are. Acknowledge it. Accept it. Embrace it.

But just because nature tells us to do something, does that mean we always should? Without sexual restraint there wouldn't be monogamy. Without dedication and discipline many significant human accomplishments wouldn't exist. Nature is a reliable and frequently wise guide—it isn't an omniscient master. It needn't be, anyway. Nietzsche was an admirer of Dostoevsky, even admitting that the Russian was "the only psychologist from whom I have anything to learn." It's not surprising then to discover that he also acknowledged the potent human desire to classify—and, even if unwittingly, help shape—the frequently nebulous experience we like to call "reality." In his *Gay Science*, Nietzsche admits, "We have arranged for ourselves a world in which we live—by positing bodies, lines, planes, causes and effects, motion and rest, form and content; without these articles of faith nobody could now endure life." At the same time, he also held that human beings can go beyond this instinctive tendency, and, in doing so, achieve a rare dignity that could potentially distinguish *homo sapiens* as a species.

I keep having the same experience and keep resisting it every time. I do not want to believe it although it is palpable: *the great majority of people lack an intellectual conscience*. Indeed, it has often seemed to me as if anyone calling for an intellectual conscience were as lonely in the most densely populated cities as if he were in a desert.

Everybody looks at you with strange eyes and goes right on handling his scales, calling this good and that evil. Nobody even blushes when you intimate that their weights are underweight; nor do people feel outraged; they merely laugh at your doubts. I mean: the great majority of people does not consider it contemptible or believe this or that and to live accordingly, without first having given themselves an account of the final and most certain reason pro and con, and without even troubling themselves about such afterward: the most gifted men and noblest women still belong to this "great majority." But what is good heartedness, refinement, or genius to me, when the person who has these virtues tolerates slack feelings in his faith and judgments and when he does not account the desire for certainty as his inmost craving and deepest distress—as that which separates the higher human beings from the lower.

Pride, the believer might hiss. What arrogance to presume that one is superior to one's fellow human beings, and doubly so because the reason for one's pride is the additional belief that one also knows better than God or society. So, Satan, the personification of human conceit in the Christian tradition, is rebuked in *Paradise Lost*: "His pride / had cast him out from Heaven, with all his host. / Of rebel angels, by whose aspiring / To set himself in glory above his peers." To which, of course, Satan replied: "Better to reign in hell than serve in Heaven." Except, what is seen as vanity in the theological context translates to humility when viewed from the purely human perspective. The non-believer in personal immortality doesn't set him or herself up as the king or queen of a new kingdom; on the contrary, they acknowledge that there *isn't* any kingdom—or, rather, that the earth, and our short time on it, is the only realm we poor spiritual serfs will likely ever know. Give the devil his due. If he's proud of his honesty, he's paid for it with his life.

(ii)

Deciding that *dead* means *dead*—that's it, that's all there is, there ain't anymore, folks—doesn't necessarily mean liking it or even accepting it. Acknowledgement isn't the same as acceptance. I acknowledge that the majority of people prefer soothing mush to stimulating art, comfortable lies to difficult truths, familiar comforts to challenging, enriching experiences, but that doesn't mean I have to accept these things. Sometimes it's healthy to hate. Anger, like envy, sloth, and sundry other supposedly deadly sins, has its appeal and its advantages if used appropriately. "Anybody can become angry—that is easy," Aristotle claimed in the *Nicomachean Ethics*, "but to be angry with the right person, and to the right degree, and at the right time, and for the right purpose, and in the right way—that is not within everybody's power and is not easy." There's an entire self-help industry predicated upon the perennial question of *How can I be happy?* Answering the question of how to be properly angry provides part of that elusive answer.

I always knew as an athlete that I could have tried harder, when, for whatever reason, something made me upset enough to skate faster, tackle the ball carrier with greater viciousness, bear down in general with a little more intensity. Later, sitting on the bench or standing on the sideline or on the way home from the game, I'd wonder why I didn't play like that all the time, why it usually took something bad, like a hard check into the boards, to wake me up and get my head in the game. I remember asking my Dad once why Larry Robinson, the Montreal Canadiens' mammoth defenceman, didn't get into fights as much as players not nearly as big as him or why he didn't throw his weight around more and intimidate the opposition.

"The other teams know to leave him alone," he said. "You don't want to poke the bear. You don't want the bear to wake up." Lou Reed was famous for inciting unease and creating conflict among the members of his various solo bands. They played better that way, he insisted. The more anxious they were, he reasoned, the more intensely they played.

Just as anger can be employed with profit to enhance life's enjoyment, it can also be utilized to prolong it. Literature's most famous paean to anger in the aid of extending the battle with mortality is, of course, written by Dylan Thomas, who encouraged the reader in "Do Not Go Gentle Into That Good Night" to rage and rage and rage some more. The initial—and undeniably healthy—response to learning that one has a potentially fatal malady like cancer is usually something akin to "I'm going to beat this disease" or "Fuck cancer." The aggressive language could partly be a case of swearing past the graveyard—an attempt to shore up one's courage in the face of a justifiably terrifying threat—but it's also an indication that the adrenaline has begun to flow and that one's mind and body are readying themselves for the difficult battle to come. Elemental sports psychology stresses the importance of positive visualization—if you want to succeed, don't think about not losing, think about winning. Weeks of exhausting, agonizing chemotherapy and radiation; months of tedious doctor visits or prolonged hospital-ization; continual anxiety and not infrequent panic over what's going to happen a year from now, a month, a week: it's necessary to see oneself as a powerful can-cer-fighting machine and not as a weak, fatally infected victim. Properly employed, anger is energy. And every successful fighter needs all the energy he or she can get.

And then one day it doesn't matter anymore. When the fight for life ends in defeat, as it always eventually must, there's still anger, but it falls to the survivors to do the raging now, and it's directed at death the devas-tating conqueror and what it did—and will always do—to those we love. Shakespeare's Cleopatra, upon Antony's death:

> The crown o' the earth doth melt. My lord!
> O, wither'd is the garland of the war,
> The soldier's ploe is fall'n! Young boys and girls
> Are level now with men. The odds is gone,
> And there is nothing left remarkable
> Beneath the visiting moon.

Who does this anger aid? No one. What is the point of it, then? There is none. How long will we feel it? For as long as we ourselves manage to stay topside.

This loud, useless *no no no* that helps to remind us that, evidence frequently to the contrary, we're more than fleshy machines created to eat, sleep, shit, and procreate. For a little while, anyway.

When it hinders more than it helps, though; when sense of worth transforms into arrogance: locating and maintaining the balance between profitable, self-manifesting anger and harmful, self-obsessed hubris is oftentimes difficult, yet essential to what might be called a good death. And since the fittest of us is always dying—even the pinkest, healthiest baby is crawling, then walking down the long road to eventual extinction—a good death is part of what constitutes a good life. The theologian Reinhold Niebuhr's "Serenity Prayer" has become best known as an Alcoholics Anonymous credo, but its applicability to the question of how much and when we should hate death is profoundly apposite:

> God, grant me the serenity to accept the things
>   I cannot change,
> The courage to change the things I can,
> And the wisdom to know the difference.

Like most sagacious advice, however, it's easier understood than practised.

The end of my grandfather's life was messy. Eighty-six years had left almost everything either not working or in constant need of medical attention in order to maintain a modicum of usage. *Nearly* everything—the doctor said his heart was in surprisingly excellent condition for a man his age and overall physical state and that there was no reason it couldn't keep busily beating for several more years. If it had been up to my grandfather or the people who cared about him, a few of those prospective years would have been gladly exchanged for less pain and being able to go to the bathroom by himself and being capable of consistently remembering the name of his fifty-five-year-old son when he turned up to visit him every day. But no one was offering to make the trade.

I was in graduate school and living in Texas during my grandfather's final years, but my mother told me that every day my dad would come home from work, shower and change his clothes, then go to the hospital to visit his father. Even over the telephone I could tell how exhausted both of my parents were (my mom was a frequent visitor too, as well as doing grandpa's laundry and any other daily duties that the staff was too busy for). Typical of someone my grandfather's advanced age and deteriorating physical condition, most of what counted for conversation at this time was the usual melancholy mix of either complaints (about his physical discomfort, about being too hot or too cold, about his difficulty sleeping) or dementia-inspired accusations (that the nurses were always turning his room light either on or off, that my dad's brother was coming in at night and stealing Grandpa's underwear and socks, that my father was his jailer keeping him in prison), but one day he told my father with something like his old matter-of-factness, like he was observing that he'd run out of razor blades, that he didn't have any reason to live anymore. "Live for me, then," my father answered back. I think he was as surprised to say it as my grandfather was to hear it. He told me that when he showed up at the usual time the following day, the nurse asked him what he'd said to his father the day before: he'd eaten all of his dinner for a change and was making jokes with the nurses and even talking to the other two patients who shared his room.

My father couldn't help but be proud of the effect he'd had, even if he knew its impetus had been more instinctive than reasoned. Of course *Live for me, then*. No matter what, number one is to survive, right? Right. Even if, as the weeks and then the months went by, Grandpa became entirely bedridden and increasingly disorientated and the big event of the day would be when the nurses turned him over in bed to avoid bedsores. He lived—because my father asked him to, and simply out of somatic habit, I suppose—for nearly another year. Not long before he died, when my father and one of my uncles were riding down in the hospital elevator after visiting hours, my uncle said, "Don't let that happen to me. I don't want to live like that." When my father got home, he made himself a strong rum and Coke and sat at the kitchen table and wondered why he felt guilty.

A few years later, by the time my uncle was hospitalized with the cancer that would eventually kill him, my father had figured out why. When the doctors decreed it was only a matter of time before my uncle's body would mercifully shut down of its own volition, and after he'd been drifting in and out of faint consciousness for several days, my father, who'd been sitting at his beside, waited until everyone else had left the room and took my uncle's hand and squeezed it, whispering in his ear, "Let it go, Gord. Remember what you said to me before, about Dad? How you didn't want it to be that way for you? Let it go. Just relax and let it go." Within an hour, he did. Who knows if my father's words had anything to do with it (or whether my uncle even heard them), but what is certain is that my father no longer thought survival alone was a good enough reason to keep living.

Susan Sontag's son David Rieff's memoir of his mother's long, losing battle with cancer, *Swimming in a Sea of Death*, is as ideationally provocative as it is emotionally moving. Sontag had not only beaten a particularly virulent form of the disease years before (advanced breast cancer that had spread into seventeen of her lymph nodes and necessitated a double mastectomy), but, early in her life, had made an "absolute decision not to be done in" by anyone or anything that stood in the way of her powerful desire for self-definition and intellectual and emotional growth. Everything that was most important to her, from her genre-defying books to her determinedly amorphous sexual orientation, were testament to her hard-won defiance. Then the cancer returned, this time in the shape of Myelodysplastic Syndrome (MDS), and Sontag did what she always did: immediately set out to achieve her clearly defined goal by systematically utilizing the same hard work, reason, and perseverance that had always previously enabled her to get what she wanted. "My mother had lived almost her entire seventy-one years believing that she was a person who would beat the odds," her son wrote, "no matter how steep they seemed." Up until this most recent illness, these traits had not only served Sontag well personally and professionally, but inspired deep admiration in others, including her son.

But this time, as a transplant failed and the cancer refused to retreat and Sontag's condition continued to deteriorate, her hard work, reason, and perseverance only meant that she spent nearly every waking moment consulting new doctors and scouring the internet and reading medical books in the hope of discovering a reason to believe that the fight hadn't been lost, that she still had a chance to defeat her disease. Increasingly, the job of her friends and family was to reassure her that the fight was worth continuing fighting. "My mother looked to those of us who were with her not just to keep telling her that she was right, and that there was real empirical basis for hope, but also to give her the reasons why this should be the case." By this point—logic being employed to substantiate the illogical—reason has become a tool of madness. "What she wanted from me," Rieff recalled, "was an adamant refusal to accept that it was even possible that she might not survive." Even Sontag's doctors, her committed allies in her long, brave, but ultimately futile battle, worried that her refusal to accept her imminent death meant she was denying herself the opportunity to properly say good-bye to her loved ones or make peace with herself (or any other clichéd bromide no less true for its seeming-sounding banality), and that there were other—the irony is painful to contemplate—more reasonable things to do with what little time remained. "If only my mother hadn't hoped so much," her son melancholically concludes. We die the way we live.

Everyone knows someone who has died of cancer; if they haven't, they will. It doesn't discriminate on the basis of age, race, or sex; it works quietly, steadily, determinedly; it destroys the lives of those afflicted as well as those who can usually only uselessly look on: cancer is the perfect assassin. It makes sense to hate cancer. Particularly when it finishes off its prey far too soon, when there's plenty of good left for its victims to do and lots of love still to give and receive. I can't say that the writer Paul Quarrington and I were close friends—we met too late in life to build the indissoluble bonds that often require the seemingly limitless time and shared travails of youth—but it felt that way, at least on my end, and that was mostly because of Paul. *Everyone* who knew Paul felt he was a close friend. It wasn't only his emotional warmth (I'm sure he had his moods, but I never saw him in one), although spotting Paul across the room at a crowded Toronto literary gathering was like catching sight of a lighthouse on a cold, foggy night. It wasn't just his well-known generosity (everyone knew he was the softest touch in town when it came to handing out over-the-top book blurbs). It wasn't merely his superior sense of humour or his honest appreciation of good books and good music or his eager enjoyment of everything good that life has to offer—it was because Paul was Paul. That he was also a committed, prolific writer—as egotistic, self-pitying, back-biting, and social-climbing a profession as exists— made him even more unique and appreciated.

Then he was diagnosed with lung cancer and was dead nine months later. In that interim I remember two things about Paul best, both of them entirely emblematic. I had a new novel out and was scheduled to read from it at that year's Eden Mills Writers Festival, an open air literary fair that takes place every fall near Guelph. The news of Paul's fatal diagnosis was wide-spread by this point, so I was surprised to see him among the crowd at my reading. It was a lovely, late September afternoon, sunny but with a soft, refreshing breeze, and the audience was spread out across the grass, some in lawn chairs they'd brought with them, most sitting on the ground. From the stage I spotted Paul, legs stretched out and sitting beside my wife and a friend, and was pleased. Mara liked Paul—liked him a lot—mostly because he was so likeable, but also because, unlike many other writers, he didn't find her any less worth knowing simply because she was a painter, not a writer, and therefore couldn't help him with his career. After the reading, when I went over to say hello, my happiness at seeing him was, I admit, off-set by the discomfort I felt. I knew he was going to die soon. *He* knew *I* knew he was going to die soon. What was I supposed to do? Ignore the topic? Impossible—that would be disingenuous to an offensive degree. If not, how then to bring the subject up? *Hey, Paul, I was really sorry to hear about the cancer and the death sentence you were given. If there's anything*—anything—*I can do...*

I needn't have worried. He shook my hand and congratulated me on the reading and the new book—for real, you could tell, none of that customary lit-crowd glad-handing—and I asked him if he wanted to watch the Sunday Night Football game with us at a bar near the hotel where we were all staying. He immediately agreed, and over the course of the night we cheered against the Dallas Cowboys and laughed a lot and told a lot of stories and drank a lot of draft beer—this, in addition to the several different exotic drinks Paul ordered and insisted we all try. At the end of the evening he assured us that he'd be at my Toronto launch a couple of weeks later, and when the night arrived, he'd kept his word.

It was a typical book launch—a hundred hurried conversations, few of them longer than "Hold on, I'll be right back"—and I didn't get a chance to speak to Paul one-on-one until the on-stage interview was over.

One of the questions from the audience was the ubi-quitous *What do you think about literary awards?* After delivering my usual line (a cribbed version of Kingsley Amis' "Prizes of all kinds are an inherently subjective, and usually nepotistic, affair; unless, of course, you win one—in that case, they're an entirely objective appraisal of what's best"), I added that it's helpful to remember that John Denver won a Grammy for best male performer, while John Prine didn't, and that time has a way of separating the aesthetic wheat from the chaff. I was on my way to the washroom and Paul had his coat on and was about to leave, and although I knew I might never see him again (I didn't), the situa-tion didn't allow for much more than congrats, thanks, take care, so long. As he did up the final buttons on his coat, though, "Don't forget," he added. "John Denver wrote some good songs too." Those were the last words he spoke to me.

Which, when he died a few months later, made me mad. Not because of what he said, but because some-one who felt it was their duty to put in a good word for John-fucking-Denver was gone, while a whole lot of other people without even a fraction of his kindness and magnanimity and grace were still alive. Which didn't make any sense, I knew. As much as I've wanted to sometimes, I've never believed that there exists some kind of cosmic keeper of the books who metes out rewards and punishment to the deserving. One of the subgenres of gospel music is the theodicy in song, the traditional "Farther Along" maybe the best-known example. My favourite version is the Byrds' rendition on their album of the same name, featuring the superbly straining, deeply emotive lead vocal of guitar-player extraordinaire Clarence White. The fact that White himself was killed by a drunk driver less than two years after the LP's release while loading out his equipment after a gig unavoidably adds extra poignancy to the song's lament over the world's inequity and its reassurance that the wrong will be righted some celestial day down the road. Clarence White and his string-bending guitar-playing genius silenced forever at age twenty-nine, even as the world continues to be subjected to yet *another* decade of the Rolling Stones, makes me mad. Makes me mad, which makes no damn difference. So I listen to Clarence White instead, the mellifluous tone of his twangy leads and soaring solos providing in sound what words fail to provide in sense: belief in true, unchanging, perfect things. "Freedom is the recognition of necessity," Friedrich Engels wrote. He'd never heard of Paul or Clarence White, and he wasn't talking about death, but he was right.

(iii)

But. But, but, but. Such an arresting little word, so much shimmering possibility in a single syllable, in one simple conjunction, in just three letters. Hope might be, as Emily Dickinson wrote, "the thing with feathers, that perches in the soul— / And sings the tune without the words— / And never stops—at all—", but without *but* hope wouldn't have a chance. *But* is the beginning of the grammar that saves. Potentially, at least.

If the metaphysical can't provide satisfactory consolation, perhaps a series of humanistic, secular-based *buts* might help. *But who would really want to live forever, anyway?* for instance. "If all the world were playing holidays, / To sport would be as tedious as to work," Shakespeare observed. Jules Renard went one further: "Imagine life without death. Every day, you would try to kill yourself." In *Gulliver's Travels*, there are the "Immortals," children born with a round mark on their foreheads who are called "Struldbruggs" and will never die. Although Gulliver is fascinated by these strange, fortunate beings, the townspeople of Luggnagg can only smirk in amusement at his awestruck envy. The Struldbruggs might be immortal, but they also age. As the centuries roll past, they lose their hair and teeth, the ability to see and hear, their memories and even the

ability to communicate effectively with successive generations because of the constantly changing nature of
language. Orwell posits in "Thoughts on the Common
Toad" that eternity would be wasted on most human
beings anyway, reflecting that "If a man cannot enjoy
the return of spring, why should he be happy in a...
Utopia?" Baseball is the only team sport without a time
clock, fun and games made potentially infinite, but
envision a game that never ended. Where's the structure? Where's the drama? Where's the washroom? I've
been waiting to go since the end of the three hundredth
inning.

Or consider the case of the *Simpsons*, for many
years not just the best program on television (paltry
praise, perhaps, but someone has to be number one),
but the most satirically insidious show ever to get away
with being on a mainstream television network (and
far-right Fox, at that), but which, after its first decade
or so (some would argue earlier), became painfully
predictable, most episodes a tired variation on "Homer
does something entertainingly stupid and Marge for-
gives him at the end because she loves him." Every
modification of this theme having been exhausted
(along with similarly stale storylines involving Bart,
Lisa, and a few other minor characters), it's not exactly
unpleasant to watch a new episode (thirty years later

and they're still making them), it's just not as entertaining or stimulating anymore. In fact, it's actually
kind of boring, something that would have seemed
unimaginable to its initial, most fervent fans.

Sameness tends to breed tedium and discontent. If
Billy Joel can cheat on Christie Brinkley, then none of us
is safe from the restlessness born of unrelieved routine,
no matter how inherently pleasurable. It's one of the
main reasons why otherwise happy couples cheat, why
accountants buy expensive sports cars they can't afford,
why people continue to believe, against overwhelming
evidence to the contrary, that if they go somewhere sufficiently far away or exotic on their vacation they'll
somehow be happy. Human beings crave strange.

But (that's the trouble with *buts*—there's usually
another one) how many people really would prefer
permanent extinction to occasional boredom? Even
everlasting boredom. Raskolnokov, in Dostoevsky's
Crime and Punishment, reflects:

> Where is it I've read that someone condemned
> to death says or thinks, an hour before his
> death, that if he had to live on some high rock,
> on such a narrow ledge that he'd only room to
> stand, and the ocean, everlasting darkness, ever-
> lasting solitude, everlasting tempest around

him, if he had to remain standing on a square yard of space all his life, a thousand years, an eternity, it were better to live so than to die at once! Only to live, to live and to live! Life, whatever it may be!

And would one necessarily be doomed to boredom? Wouldn't an infinite amount of time mean an infinite number of possibilities? If, for example, after a couple of hundred years as a novelist, what would stop one from doing an occupational about-face and trying out what it would be like to dedicate oneself to something a little less self-absorbing—becoming a firefighter, say, or an elementary schoolteacher? And if after a few decades one decided that giving really isn't better than receiving, one could always return to the sedentary solitariness of the writer's life, with the added bonus of having gained some valuable first-hand experience to take back to one's desk. One of the disadvantages of being an author is the difficulty of mastering one's craft and the resultant need to spend the majority of one's life sitting in front of a computer screen. With an infinite amount of time, however, getting out into the world and getting one's hands experientially dirty wouldn't be a problem. One could have one's art-for-art's sake cake and eat it too.

There are as many other *buts*, however, as there are reasons to want them to exist. Such as: Okay, I myself might one day die, never to literally be me ever again, but a part of me *will* live on, through my children. But even if we grant that your surname will survive for a few further generations, or that one's receding hairline and genetic tendency toward type 1 diabetes might be passed down to your children's children's children, or that your picture will sit framed, if usually ignored, on your grandchildren's living room mantle piece, it's still not you. A name, a disease, a photograph: these aren't the same thing as being alive. And if your primary reason for procreating isn't the desire to experience the unique role of mother or father, but, instead, to propagate your personal identity (however fruitlessly, as noted), you do so because you've tacitly admitted that your own life simply isn't memorable enough to get the job done. Bertrand Russell, from *The Conquest of Happiness*:

> To be happy in this world, especially when youth is past, it is necessary to feel oneself not merely an isolated individual whose day will soon be over, but part of the stream of life flowing on from first germ to the remote and unknown future...A man who is capable of some great and remarkable achievement which

sets its stamp upon the future may gratify this feeling through this work, but for men and women who have no exceptional gifts, the only way to do so is through children.

Procreation as self-perpetuation: pointless *and* crudely utilitarian.

And the dead sometimes *do* live on after their bodies have disappeared—when their art has not. I remember reading about the death of singer-songwriter John Stewart in the newspaper while riding the bus and thinking it was sad. Stewart's music had been a recent enthusiasm, particularly his second and best album, *California Bloodlines,* an unheralded linchpin of the entire late-sixties country-rock movement. A moment later, while looking out the window, I thought, *That's bullshit. I'm not sad at all.* Stewart hadn't made a good album in twenty-five years, so it wasn't as if fans like me would likely be losing out on any more must-hear music, and while his wife and children and friends must have been understandably devastated, I'd never even seen him perform live, let alone knew him as an individual, so it wasn't as if I was going to miss him personally. What I *did* know and love, however—the music—hadn't gone anywhere, was still lying in the black plastic grooves of one of my three vinyl copies of

California Bloodlines, waiting to be liberated from its record sleeve so it could deliver its country-folk inflected magnificence one more time.

But even if one does have those "exceptional gifts" that Russell writes of and that John Stewart possessed, and one is undeniably admired and made memorable, so what? Immortality doesn't do you much good when you're six feet under. Besides, reputations wane, dynasties fizzle out, the famous become the forgotten, today's award-winning bestseller becomes tomorrow's tiresome old remainder, and even the earth itself will one day be a dead, deserted rock. "Vanity of vanities, says the Preacher, vanity of vanity! All is vanity. What does man gain by all the toil at which he toils under the sun?" Nothing, nada, butkis, zilch.

Regardless of whether we acknowledge that, enthusiastic procreator or immortality-obsessed creator or not, we must die, there's also the argument that says death is nothing to fear; in fact, in certain cases, it is to be welcomed. Plato makes this case in the *Apology,* when Socrates argues that either one of two things happens when we die: either consciousness continues to exist in one form or another, which sounds just fine to him since he'll be able to have some very stimulating conversations with all of the great thinkers of the past, or death means oblivion and the cessation of consciousness, which Socrates doesn't find frightening because, being unconscious, he would be forever free of all pain and suffering.

Given the collective degree of human misery and general unhappiness at any point in human history, it's not surprising that this argument has been particularly popular throughout the ages. "There the wicked cease from troubling," the author of Job in the Old Testament councils, "and there the weary be at rest." Similarly, from Spencer's *Faerie Queene*: "Sleepe after toyle, port after stromie seas, / Ease after warre, death after life does greatly please." And while it's impossible to ascribe any particular philosophical belief to gloriously protean Shakespeare, death as a merciful panacea for life's enduring pain—physical and otherwise— appears frequently throughout his plays, as when Macbeth notes the cruel irony that the murder of Duncan has brought the deceased the happiness and peace that he and Lady Macbeth now so clearly lack:

> Better be with the dead
> Whom we, to gain our peace, have sent to peace,
> Than on the torture of the mind to lie
> In restless ecstasy. Duncan is in his grave.
> After life's fitful fever, he sleeps well;
> Treason has done his worst; nor steel nor poison,

> Malice domestic, foreign levy, nothing
> Can touch him further.

In *Cymbeline* it's Guiderius who encourages the anxious reader, frightened of death but weary of life, to

> Fear no more the heat o' the sun
> Nor the furious winter's rages;
> Thou thy worldly task hast done,
> Home art gone and ta'en thy wages.

My own experience of intense physical discomfort has been fortunately narrow (this will change, of course, as I grow older), that sudden, middle-of-the-night onset of a searing kidney stone already alluded to the worst pain I've yet had to endure. Lying on the hallway hospital bed waiting for the morphine to do its job—and after the nurse said she couldn't administer any more for another half an hour, she was sorry, I'd just have to put up with the pain as best as I could—I felt as if I understood for the first time how a person could possibly choose death over life if it meant the immediate cessation of physical suffering. I didn't want to die—it was only a kidney stone, after all—but I didn't want to be alive, either, not while I hurt so much. "For all the happiness mankind can gain," John Dryden wrote, "Is not in pleasure, but in rest from pain." A permanent solution to a temporary problem might not be logical, but sometimes it certainly makes sense. Even those fatally or near-fatally ill and dedicated to fighting for a few precious extra years or even months can grow exhausted with the grinding tedium of terminal illness as much as any pain, with the never-ending need to scrupulously DO THIS and DON'T DO THAT, of interminable hospital visits and never doing the things that had previously defined them, of seeming to live on solely in order to fight their omnipresent disease. Dr. Johnson, himself no stranger to physical woes, referred to death as "kind nature's signal of retreat."

The idea of death can also be comforting if seen as the great leveller, particularly to those who, living in societies that frequently divide its members into the haves and have-nots, find themselves among the unfortunate latter. In Guiderius' same speech, he reminds the reader that "Golden lads and girls all must, / As chimney-sweepers come to dust," echoing Horace when he wrote that "Pale death, with impartial step, knocks at the poor man's cottage and the palaces of kings." Then there was Salon, who went even further, viewing death as something not to be feared but welcomed—in fact one can't go any further: "Call no man happy until he's dead."

Variations on Socrates' overall argument run throughout antiquity, providing the foundation for many an illustrious *but*. Epicurus' is typical, with the emphasis on the idea that worrying about death is the only way it can actually hurt you, since when you're dead you won't know it, and how can something you don't experience cause you pain?

Accustom yourself to believing that death is nothing to us, for good and evil imply the capacity for sensation, and death is the priva-tion of all sentience; therefore, a correct understanding that death is nothing to us makes the mortality of life enjoyable, not by adding to life a limitless time, but by taking away the yearning for immortality. For life has no terrors for him who has thoroughly under-stood that there are no terrors for him in ceasing to live. Foolish, therefore, is the man who says that he fears death, not because it will pain when it comes, but because it pains in the prospect. Whatever causes no annoyance when it is present causes only a groundless pain in the expectation. Death, therefore, the most awful of evils, is nothing to us, seeing that, when we are, death is not come, and when death is come, we are not. It is nothing, then, either to the living or to the dead, for with the living it is not and the dead exist no longer.

"Loss is nothing else but change, and change is Nature's delight," Marcus Aurelius assures the reader. Or if one prefers one's cosmic consolation a little more homespun, there's Mark Twain, who claimed, "I do not fear death. I had been dead for billions and billions of years before I was born, and had not suffered the slightest inconvenience from it."

And the argument does make sense, it could be true, there is an undeniable degree of logical legitimacy to it. So why, then, ultimately, doesn't it make one feel much better? It's because, I believe, we know from experience that any frightened animal seeks safety. Pursued by a predator, it runs and hides. Human beings are no different—are animals as well—and do the same thing, although the predator is often lurking not around the corner but within our own minds. We also look for an escape route, a way out, something to save us. So we turn to consoling arguments that reassure us that in death we won't feel any sorrow, disappointment, or pain. That we won't know that we're dead when we're dead. And so on.

You won't find the distinction in any philosophy textbook, but there's daytime truth and there's night-time truth. Daytime truth is bright and buoyant and certainly plausible and what we want to believe. Night-time truth is overheated-bedroom hard darkness and 3:27 a.m. unavoidable. It's not to an epistemologist, but, predictably, a poet, we turn to in order to understand—i.e. experience—the dreadful difference. Specifically, Shakespeare, in *Macbeth:*

> To-morrow, and to to-morrow, and to-morrow,
> Creeps in this petty pace from day to day,
> To the last syllable of recorded time;
> And all our yesterdays have lighted fools
> The way to dusty death. Out, out, brief candle!
> Life's but a walking shadow.

A "walking shadow." This is as good a description of what depression feels like as any other.

(iv)

You don't need to think about death to be depressed. Life provides plenty of opportunities all by itself. But death depression is a special kind of sad. *Impending-*

death depression. Claudio, speaking to his sister Isabella, in *Measure for Measure*:

> The weariest and most loathed worldly life
> That age, ache, penury, and imprisonment
> Can lay on nature, is a paradise
> To what we fear of death.

Of course, there are also those who never suspected death would come for them so soon and were therefore unable to anticipate, prepare for, and perhaps even understand their own mortal end. The blindsided car crash victim. The fatal casualty of a sudden, violent crime. The recipient of a somnolent heart attack or stroke. Certainly a case can be made that remaining ignorant of one's imminent death is an enviable condition. My maternal grandmother died in her favourite living room chair during her customary post-supper snooze, my grandfather only out of the room long enough to wash up their few dirty dishes and make her her usual cup of tea before returning to find her dead. "They say the best thing you can hope for is to die in your sleep," he said to me at the funeral, not sure, I think, whether he was one of "them." What's gained by escaping the awful anxiety of wondering whether this will be your last day as yourself, next stop undifferentiated permanent oblivion, is offset, however, by being lopped off from life like a careless squirrel squashed by a car in the street. Animals are an even more extreme example of this special sort of ignorance—they suffer pain and know fear, but aren't aware of their own mortality. Which is fine for them. But we're not intellectually insentient animals. We're human beings. We're constructed differently. And, as John Stuart Mill argued, "It is better to be a human being dissatisfied than a pig satisfied; better to be Socrates dissatisfied than a fool satisfied. And if the fool, or the pig, are of a different opinion, it is because they only know their side of the question."

But: *nothing without a price*. Of all of adulthood's sweet and sour life lessons, none is more elemental or inescapable. Saturday night must be paid for with Sunday morning. Fortunately (or unfortunately), you may not be Socrates, but you're not a pig either—you're a *Homo sapiens*. And, in addition, you're also the only animal on planet earth who knows it's going to die and is never coming back and there isn't a damn thing you or anyone else can do about it. Congratulations on that whole *Homo sapiens* thing. Enjoy those opposable thumbs and well-developed frontal lobes because they sure don't come cheap.

One of the first things my friend Paul did after receiving the fatal final verdict on what he initially suspected was a spring tulip allergy (a tulip allergy!) but turned out be stage four lung cancer, was to go for a long walk alone along the Scarborough Bluffs and, in his own words, "have a good cry." Self-pity is among the least attractive of human tendencies—"Self pity is easily the most destructive of the non-pharmaceutical drugs," the novelist John Gardner wrote, "it is addictive, gives momentary pleasure and separates the victim from reality"—but, faced with looming annihilation, no one can be begrudged a hearty bout of woe-is-me. If there was ever a time to wail *Why Me? It's not fair! No one knows how I feel!* this would be it. As unhealthy as prolonged self-pity is, it at least indicates that the sufferer still cares enough about the outside world to insist upon making one's sad case known and feels sufficiently indignant to blame someone or something for what's been done to them.

To the severely depressed individual, however, anger is as rare as happiness, life's luminosity reduced to a pinprick of light—everything that's seen, heard, felt, and thought becoming everything that's wrong with existence. Deep depression means not caring anymore. When an animal stops grooming itself, it's getting ready to die. Someone else can tend to an ailing person's hygiene and physical care, but only the patient can desire to go on living. Six months to the day before his death from heart disease, the critic Edmund Wilson, worn down by assorted physical pains as well as a disheartening inability to perform the simplest of everyday tasks, like take a book down from the shelf or go to the bathroom without great effort (this was a man who used to order five martinis at a time and liked to learn foreign languages as a way of relaxing), noted in his journal:

> When I look back, I feel quite definitely div-
> ided from my earlier self, who cared about
> things in a way I no longer do. All that com-
> edy and conflict of human activity—one gets
> to feel cut off from all that. One cannot even
> imagine any more the time when one partici-
> pated. One ought perhaps to have died before
> reaching this point, when one still had the
> illusion...

It might be an illusion to believe that it matters whether or not the truth is acknowledged, that good art should be preferable to bad, that ethical fairness be practised— it might even be an illusion that ideals such as truth, beauty, and justice aren't simply human-constructed chimera—but caring about these sometimes slippery conceptions is what human beings do. When we stop caring about them, we cease being human.

In their place is death. Incomprehensible, omnipresent, indomitable death. "And a handful of dust has closed up all its beauty," Sophocles wrote in *Antigone*. Here's the titular character of Tolstoy's novella *The Death of Ivan Ilych*, not long before he dies:

> For three whole days, during which time did not exist for him, he struggled in that black sack into which he was being thrust by an invisible, restless force. He struggled as a man condemned to death struggles in the hands of the executioner, knowing that he cannot save himself. And every moment he felt that despite all his efforts he was drawing nearer and nearer to what terrified him.

Near the end of his life, if sufficiently mellowed by enough malt whisky, the physically frail, nursing-home marooned, octogenarian Samuel Beckett was known to sing an old Irish hymn that was the favourite of the main character of his play *Krapp's Last Tape*: "Now the day is over, / Night is drawing nigh, / Shadows of the evening/Steal across the sky."

Pain, whether physical or mental or a crushing combination of the two, focuses the mind, makes almost everything except for its relief irrelevant. Desperate for some kind of respite from the encroaching darkness one feels is in danger of engulfing oneself, there's a craving for the solidity of the inanimate, a desire to be attached to—to *be*—something more stabilizing and enduring than one's own fragile, shattered self. To be, yet also not to be—that is the answer. Anything other than being what one has become.

Where there's humour, there's hope. Being able to imaginatively stand outside of a situation and see—and laugh at—its absurdity means not being imprisoned by the self-absorption that's an implicit part of the severely depressed state. If one can still laugh—especially if one can still laugh at oneself—depression's shadow hasn't entirely eclipsed the totality of the individual. A little over two years before his death, Evelyn Waugh was certainly depressed, but not so much that he couldn't, even in the midst of detailing to a correspondent why he wouldn't make a good dinner guest, see the dark comedy in his increasing decrepitude:

> The truth is that I am no longer sortable—deaf, toothless, without appetite, reduced to extreme exhaustion... I should only be a bore and a

burden...I can only be regarded as a ghost. People get a macabre pleasure in observing the decay of their contemporaries. That is the only pleasure I can hope to give the assembled company.

By the time he finally did become more ghost than man, suffering a massive heart attack while in the washroom, in the process of staggering from the toilet smashing his head on the door handle, such epistolary wit was painfully, conspicuously rare.

If depression is loathing life, suicide is murdering it. Tired of waiting for the pain to stop, one simply stops the pain. Permanently. *Simply* seems out of place here—what could be more profound than ending one's existence?—but most suicides act because they can't tolerate the pain any longer and can't see that it will ever abate. For all of the Romantic rhetoric that is often attached to it, suicide is instinctual. The novelist Wilfred Sheed: "The rational man may talk a good game about suicide, but reason must give way to obsession and finally squalor before he can actually do it." Obsession is instinct made insane. No one kills him or herself because they *want* to; they *have* to.

In a sense, every death by suicide is in response to a death sentence; if not because of a fatal medical pronouncement, then because the individual himself or herself has confirmed life as lethally noxious and a swift exit the only sensible prescription. The deaths by suicides that I've personally known have belonged to the latter category, and I believe that, in their own minds, it was as if a doctor's terminal diagnosis had been delivered from on high and that suicide was the less painful of the two options. Many people who die by suicide don't leave notes, but Hunter S. Thompson did write one (it's almost impossible for a writer to resist a potential reader), and it's instructive not because of what it reveals about the particular details of his decision to take his own life, but what it so coolly, cogently suggests about the archetypal suicidal mindset. "No More Games. No More Bombs. No More Walking. No More Fun. No More Swimming. 67. That is 17 years past 50. 17 more than I needed or wanted. Boring. I am always bitchy. No Fun—for anybody. 67. You are getting Greedy. Act your old age. Relax— This won't hurt."

What's most apparent in the case of the majority of those who die by suicide is the desire to put an end to the pain that has made life unendurable or, as in Thompson's case, joylessly pointless (or, frequently, symbiotically, both). Less obviously, there's also usually a discernible calm after the decision to die has been reached, the furious energy that feeds even the most listless depression replaced by an almost contented acquiescence. Death has gone from being feared and shunned to esteemed and accepted. The battle might have been lost, but at least it's over. And then, finally, peace.

(v)

Checkers; an argument; your own life: no one likes to lose. Not all losses are created equal, however. No more life means not only no more games or important, argument-clinching points, but no more you. For now, forever, for what it's worth and whatever it was or wasn't. But death is also defeat's defeat. And for the terminally ill, the perpetually suffering, the hospital-bed-condemned, it can also be a veiled victory, death emerging late in the game as an unexpected, merciful redeemer.

Because, in its most advanced state, it reduces consciousness to a minimum and allows the afflicted to drift off into death's embrace in a relatively benign manner, pneumonia used to be referred to as "the old man's friend." The death-obsessed sentiments of Philip Larkin's "Aubade"—perhaps the finest contemporary poem on the subject of death—weren't assumed for prosody's sake; the poet was a lifelong hypochondriac whose oeuvre abounds with dread-ridden disquisitions on impending mortality (his and everyone else's). After the poem's publication, Larkin received several letters from appreciative readers, one of whom, a seventy-two-year-old woman, wrote that she'd experienced the death dread he writes so well of in "Aubade," but claimed that she didn't feel that way anymore because the body prepares one for death. Larkin was intrigued, but skeptical. This skepticism lasted until—his body worn down by the cancer that would kill him, his brain numbed by the drugs that made his pain tolerable—he was able to utter his last words to the nurse holding his hand not long before he stopped breathing, "I am going to the inevitable." Our bodies know things our brains alone don't.

Even if we're not pinned to our beds by death's cold, indefatigable grip and we're allowed to grow old without undue injury or disease, our judicious bodies unswervingly assist us in the long process of learning to become accustomed to our gradual physical deterioration. Cicero, from his classic treatise on aging, *De Senectute*: "I am wise in that I follow that good guide nature; it is not likely, when she has written the rest of the play so well, that she should, like a lazy playwright, skimp the last act." Nature is such a good guide, it even assists us in coming to better accept the idea of our eventual non-existence. Montaigne:

[W]hen we are led by nature's hand down a gentle and virtually imperceptible slope, bit by bit, one step at a time, she rolls us into this wretched state and makes us familiar with it; so that we feel no shock when youth dies within us, which in essence and in truth is a harder death than the complete death of a languishing life or the death of old age; inasmuch as the leap is not so cruel from a painful life to no life as from a sweet and flourishing life to a grievous and painful one.

One day there's a grey hair—My God, can you believe it? Me? Going grey?—and then, when another couple of silver strands appear a month or so afterward, it doesn't seem so shocking somehow, seems just, well, *you*. A year later and a touch of grey has become a head full of silver, and what do you know, it sort of suits you, doesn't it? Time and nature are excellent guides, the unimaginable made humdrum one educative day at a time.

I like my life. I'm lucky, I've earned it, I enjoy it. One of the things I enjoy most is when my work is going well, when I'm in a productive groove and the words are adding up and they're good words, too, sentences snapping to attention as soon as they're assembled and narrative momentum and sustaining structure somehow miraculously emerging from what once seemed just inchoate words and more words. I also like the work-play symbiosis that occurs when industry and inspiration come together during the day and a bottle of wine, a little THC, and a couple hours of headphone-assisted music listening await me at night. The latter is looked forward to with anticipation; the former is looked back upon with gratification, neither activity as enjoyable without the existence of the other. I feel most alive when I'm on a roll with a new book. It feels as if I'm one of those lucky people I used to read about in biographies when I was young who knew that what they were doing was what they were supposed to be doing. Like I said, I'm lucky.

Which is what makes the idea of being either too old or too sick to do it anymore (or being dead, and doing nothing) so frightening. Between books is when I tend to get into trouble—goodbye supporting sense of purpose and ongoing feeling of aesthetic delight, hello what the hell am I supposed to do with myself besides let the field lie fallow and make enough money to live on and wonder when the next book will reveal itself and demand to be written—and from where I'm standing right now, being old and/or infirm seems like one long between-book snooze. Outliving my need or ability to work doesn't sound like much of a life. A life, maybe, but not a reason to live.

But then I remember what it's like when I have the flu. I don't care about books, mine or anyone else's, I don't care about the post-work glow that cheap booze and expensive records provide, I don't care about maintaining a sense of meaning in my life, I don't care about death meaning no more novels or wine or weed or music—all I want is to climb underneath the heavy blankets of my bed and go to sleep. Maybe, I remind myself, this is what the end of life will feel like: not having something to devotedly care about won't matter much because I won't care. About anything. Not surprisingly, Montaigne entertained much the same thought, nearly six hundred years earlier:

> Nature lends us her hand and gives us courage...I find that I have much more trouble digesting this resolution to die when I am in health than when I have a fever. Inasmuch as I no longer cling so hard to the good things of life when I begin to lose the use and pleasure of them, I come to view death with much less frightened eyes.

For most of us, our eventual acceptance of death won't be a matter of intellectual assent; it will be what our bodies demand. And if there is an element of cerebral cognizance, it will only be because we possess the wisdom to recognize the critical role our body plays in such a "decision," as the 71-year-old Thomas Jefferson did when writing to his friend, the 78-year-old John Adams: "But our machines have now been running seventy or eighty years, and we must expect that, worn as they are, here a pivot, there a wheel, now a pinion, next a spring, will be giving away; and however we may tinker them up for a while, all will at length surcease motion."

We'll simply know it's time for us to stop.

PART THREE

PART THREE

Knowing death at least a little bit better, what have we gained, how are we better off? *Are* we better off? If there's any truth at all in the overused proverb *Ignorance is bliss*, then it has to apply to this seminal subject, doesn't it? The surgeon and author Sherwin B. Nuland argued that no, it doesn't. Vehemently *no*. In fact, his opposition to such an idea provides the thesis of his book *How We Die: Reflections on Life's Final Chapter*. Nuland's expressed goal is "to present [death] in its biological and clinical reality, as seen by those who are witness to it" (such as himself, a doctor for over thirty years). In sometimes explicit anatomical detail, Nuland elucidates the most common ways human beings die (the stoppage of circulation; the inadequate transportation of oxygen to tissues; the flickering out of brain functions; the failure of organs; the destruction of vital centres) as they manifest themselves in the cancers, strokes, heart attacks, traumas, et cetera, that get written on our death certificates. His goal isn't merely descriptive, however, but also prescriptive:

> A realistic sense of what is to be expected
> [when we're dying] serves as a defense against
> the unrestrained conjurings of warrantless fears
> and the terror that one is somehow not doing
> things right. Each disease is a distinctive pro-
> cess—it carries its own particular kind of
> destructive work within a framework of highly
> specific patterns. When we are familiar with the
> patterns of the illness that afflicts us, we disarm
> our imaginings... Better to know what dying is
> like, and better to make choices that are most
> likely to avert the worst of it. What cannot be
> averted can usually at least be mitigated.

Be aware, be prepared, make the best death you can.

Which makes sense, which is good to know, which might come in handy one distressing day down the road. But I've always been more of a What-has-knowledge-done-for-me-lately? kind of person. Meaning, how can death—understanding it, accepting it, learning from it—improve the quality of my life? The motto that will often be found hanging on a morgue wall is *Hic est locus ubi mors gaudet succurso vitaa* (This is the place where death rejoices to come to the aid of life). The pathologist and the medical researcher regularly util-ize death in the hope of helping human beings live healthier and longer. Our task is similar, and, I would argue, even more important: to use death to assist us in learning how to live better and be happier. Because we can certainly use all of the help we can get in those two departments.

I'm selfish. I'm not the only one who is and there are others who are more so than me, but none of that makes me any less self-centred. Which, if one is talking about being somebody who has a tendency to take the last piece of pizza or who never replaces the milk when they've emptied the bag, isn't that significant a character flaw. Occasionally annoying to others, perhaps, but not a momentous personal limitation and certainly not a noteworthy impediment to personal happiness and growth. But not only wanting what one can't have, but wanting what it's plainly unreasonable to even desire, is not only futile, it's embarrassingly puerile.

Like the wish that one wasn't old. That one could be the person one has grown to become yet simultaneously still possess the in-the-pink physiological attributes of one's younger self. "Youth is wasted on the young," Oscar Wilde famously remarked (or George Bernard Shaw—its origin is as obscure as its profundity is obvious), a truism whose veracity is only wholly revealed to those old enough to feel its sagacious sting. Only now—in my early fifties—do I feel as if I'm finally figuring out how to live the way I always wanted, that the right mix of zestful restlessness *and* prudent patience, of necessary individual independence *and* collective connection and responsibility, of experiential omnivorousness *and* cosmological ambivalence, of eagerly looking forward to what's next *and* contentedly being here right now are finally beginning to coalesce. Not perfectly, and certainly not consistently, but at least these very different elements know who each other are now and have begun to get along. It's a good start.

A good start that's come along just as it's become impossible to ignore the fact that I'm beginning to wind down to an eventual full stop. Barring any unexpected major illnesses or accidents (as if anyone ever *expects* either of these things) and taking into consideration family genealogy and long-term, late-night lifestyle habits, I'm assuming I've got a couple more decades to go, tops, by which time I'll probably be just starting to refer to myself as an adult without any detectable irony. It feels like—and will feel even more like, I'm sure—finally getting my driver's licence while simultaneously developing an incurable case of motion sickness. Youth is wasted on the young, indeed.

Age makes its demands, and they're frequently the kind you can't refuse. I'm a writer who stopped drinking caffeine and eating most forms of refined sugar several years ago (gasoline to the fire of my obsessive-compulsive disorder), two of the staples of my daily writing stint for nearly two decades. It might be hyperbole, but it might not be either: I'm not sure I would have ever even become a writer without both of these compositional aids. Getting good at something (or determining that you're not good at it and never will be, probably just as valuable) isn't a mystery: you simply do it a lot. *A lot.* Over and over and over. Inspiration and dedication are wonderful and necessary things, but both can use a chemical kickstart once in awhile. I now have to supply that kick with a cup of decaffeinated tea and a piece of fresh fruit, and, believe me, the *au naturel* boost simply isn't the same. Growing old doesn't mean you don't have plenty of options anymore; rather, that the tenor of your choices have changed. Instead of, say, wondering whether you want to be a dental hygienist or a circus acrobat, you're more likely to have to decide between a lifetime of chamomile tea or incipient mental illness.

And that's where the selfishness comes in. And must be combated. Having had my turn at being Teflon tough and springy sprightly and delighting in everything nourishing new, now it's simply someone else's turn. That restless queue behind you is an increasingly large percentage of the population pushing their way to the front, ready for their opportunity to be young and vital and resilient just like you once upon a time were. Your mother's voice in your head should be all the philosophical elucidation you need: *It just wouldn't be fair any other way.* "It must require an inordinate share of vanity and presumption too," the poet Heine wrote, "after enjoying so much that is good and beautiful on earth, to ask the Lord [or nature] for immortality in addition to it all." Renard, after reading over some of his old letters late in life, observed how "you become aware that you have, after all, loved, and that it is natural for life to pass and, even, for it to end." It's not much different from what your parents attempted to impart to you all those years ago: part of being a grown-up is accepting that you don't always get what you want. So don't be a baby. And speaking of, don't forget: every infant is an old man or old woman in disguise.

And in spite of frustratingly failing eyesight and creaky bones on damp days and an occasionally sore back and shortness of breath accompanying what used to get done so easily, sometimes it's even preferable to be an old man. I wish I was who I am right now except twenty years younger. Who wouldn't? But twenty years back, while I might have been stronger and healthier and with a full head of hair, I wasn't the author of a dozen books—and for much of my life, being a writer was the only thing I ever wanted to be—and as good a husband and friend and son (if still clearly lacking in all three categories) as I am now. It's that fair thing again: if you want to produce a shelf full of books and become a better person, that takes, among other things, time— the time that is called your life. Adult happiness is being satisfied with that tradeoff. Earlier, I quoted from memory Philip Larkin's last words. After I was done writing for the day I went to the bookshelf and took down his biography to verify the quote. I'd got it right, word for word. The twenty-five-year-old me would have been impressed. I'm pretty sure he would have swapped his thirty-two inch waist for that slightly softer old guy's bibliographical memory and plump oeuvre.

Grasping some of the benefits of aging is easier than seeing the glass half-empty—and not half-full—of death. Even death's sometimes merciful cessation of pain and suffering is a decidedly mixed blessing, since the pain and suffering aren't the only things that stop: so does the sufferer. Permanently. It's a little like someone who suffers from a rare skin disease that doesn't allow them to step into the sun winning a week's paid vacation at a Florida beach resort in August. On the one hand...

But death does have something to offer the living— something potentially life-changing—if only we accept its admittedly steep terms of transaction. In return for acknowledging that when we cease breathing, we cease existing—no sophistic ifs, ands, or buts about it—we're given the gift of potentially better recognizing the fragility, the uniqueness, the preciousness of existence. And while recognizing death's omnipotent imminence isn't a guarantee of a deeper appreciation of life (when a friend's father was diagnosed with terminal lung cancer and told he had six months to live, his first words to his son as they exited the hospital were "Well, at least I can start smoking again"), it is possible to utilize such a recognition as an existential wake-up call.

Wilko Johnson, the kamikaze guitar player and principal songwriter in the British pub rock band Dr. Feelgood, experienced a dramatic re-evaluation of his life after learning of his own fatal diagnosis:

> When...the doctor told me "You've got cancer" it was quite plain it was an inoperable thing, there was nothing they could do [but somehow Johnson felt] an elation of spirit...You're walking along and suddenly you're vividly alive. You're looking at the trees and the sky and everything and it's just "whoa." I am actually a miserable person. I've spent most of my life moping in depressions and things, but this has all lifted.

Later, after an experimental treatment allowed doctors to remove a three-pound tumour (as well as Johnson's pancreas, spleen, and part of his stomach) and he was eventually deemed cancer-free, the newly gained euphoria of being alive still hadn't worn off. "I was supposed to be dead," Johnson said, "but here I am doing things like walking up the road to meet me mate for lunch. Enjoying a fry-up in the caff, looking out over the Thames Delta, watching the sun dancing on the water. Ha. Every day is filled with wonderful feelings."

Johnson's case is as rare as it is ideal: little effort is needed to envisage one's non-existence when one has been informed by a medical authority that one is going to die; and no eventual outcome could have been more providential. Not many people, however, get to have their inspirational mortality cake and eat it too. Most of us have to try our best to imagine the unimaginable in order to better savour the sweet ephemerality of life, to assist us in our ongoing attempt, as Shelley put it in his *A Defence of Poetry*, to "strip the veil of familiarity from the world" and "purge from our inward sight the film of familiarity which obscures from us the wonder...of the universe, after it has been annihilated in our minds by the recurrence of impressions blunted by reiteration." Even if we have plenty to eat and a well-shingled roof over our heads and plenty of family and friends and things to be thankful for, it's undeniable that habit, familiarity, routine, and repetition do tend to have a way of eroding our appreciation and enjoyment of life. And what's the point of being happy if you don't know it?

The capacity for deep, authentic happiness is as much a hard-earned skill as mastering a musical instrument: it requires no less intelligence, patience, and commitment. The Kayagatsati Sutta is a Pali Buddhist Sutta which attempts to aid individuals in their quest for the desired state of mindfulness by, among other things, advocating meditation on the impermanence of the human body via contemplating corpses in their various states of decomposition: "Furthermore, as if he were to see a corpse cast away in a charnel ground—one day, two days, three days dead—bloated, livid, and festering, he applies it to this very body, 'This body, too: Such is its nature, such is its future, such is its unavoidable fate.'" One doesn't have to be a practising Buddhist to benefit from this sort of measured rumination since at its core it's simply an attempt to aid in the heightening of one's awareness of life's undeniably ethereal, transparently tragic, manifold magnificence.

One also doesn't have to be a back-to-the-woods advocate or agrarian fantasist to suspect that some things—some elemental things—were sacrificed when the majority of the Western world migrated to cities over the last two centuries. I have a lot of faults, but nostalgic sentimentality isn't one of them. I don't tweet or text, I wouldn't know how to post a picture on Instagram if I was inclined (I'm not), I don't even own a cellphone, but I'd never exchange the chance for a return to a quieter, stiller, less technologically fraught era if it also meant living without YouTube, Zoloft, or my Seinheiser headphones. But it's undeniable that most rural dwellers possess an organic understanding of the life cycle that urbanites don't. Whether because of a simple proximity to nature's ancient lessons in tenuousness and transience or by virtue of routinely witnessing the birth, life, and death of farm animals, people who live off or close to the land tend to view death much more matter-of-factly. My mother's older brother Gerald died when he was three. It was the early 1940s and rural Ontario and her family were poor and didn't have medical insurance and he perished from whooping cough. The family was obviously sad, but it was also wintertime and the ground was too hard to bury the body, so they wrapped Gerald in a blanket and stored him in the barn until spring arrived. When the weather warmed and the earth became pliable again they removed him from the barn and buried him in the cemetery. "Death is the normal state," Renard wrote in his journal. "We make too much of life."

Although Bertrand Russell was as far from being a Buddhist or a farm dweller as any mathematician/logician/philosopher born of British aristocrats who also happened to be an atheistic empiricist can be, his essentially tragic understanding of human existence was predicated on a similar stoical awareness and acceptance of death:

> I believe that when I die I shall rot, and nothing of my ego will survive. I am not young and I love life. But I should scorn to shiver with terror at the thought of annihilation. Happiness is nonetheless true happiness because it must come to an end, nor do thought and love lose their value because they are not everlasting. Many a man has borne himself proudly on the scaffold; surely the same pride should teach us to think truly about man's place in the world. Even if the open windows of science at first make us shiver after the cosy indoor warmth of traditional humanizing myths, in the end the fresh air brings vigour, and the great spaces have a splendour of their own.

There it is, if by implication only. The *T* word. Tragedy. There's no avoiding what it means to view existence as sketched out above and to live according to its dictates. And tragedy is not something North Americans tend to do well. Or are even comfortable with. One need look no further than its bastardization in everyday speech to get a taste of its malformed tenor. "Didn't you hear? He got killed in a head-on car collision. What a tragedy." Whenever something bad happens, it's a tragedy, and if it happens to someone blameless, young, or someone you knew personally, it's more than that, it's what's called a *real* tragedy (or some equally emphatic adjectival variation thereof). "She was the mother of three small children, too. It's *such* a tragedy."

In many ways, North Americans are good at happiness. Desiring it, demanding it, dreaming up new schemes of achieving it, even going so far as codifying it (in the American Declaration of Independence, guaranteeing its citizens the right to pursue it). This shouldn't be surprising, as the entire American democratic experiment was predicated upon a basic self-improvement principle: things are okay over here (in Europe), but over there (in North America) they'll be even better. This helps explain our obsession with what's new. Thirty years ago, sports/entertainment stadium X was state of the art, a fresh source of civic pride, the revitalizing jewel of the surrounding community. Today, it's technologically behind the times, increasingly economically

unfeasible, an architecturally shabby eyesore. So bring
in the dynamite and the bulldozers and hit up the citizen suckers for another three-quarters of a billion
dollars in tax money and soon we'll have a stadium that
will be the envy of everyone. For another couple of decades, at least. Old churches and all the rotting rest of it
are for visiting overseas when you're retired and haven't
got anything better to do.

One aspect of happiness we're not so good at is
achieving it. No continent has more expensive shiny
stuff, more diverting ways to ceaselessly amuse itself,
more industries dedicated to delivering the self-
gratification goods than North America. Happiness
itself, however, tends to remain elusive. Other societies
often look at us and our prolonged peace and prosper-
ity (admittedly, not for all members) and can only
wonder at our interminably whining ways. Not as fortunate as we are, they avoid the misfortune of expecting
everything to always turn out all right and feeling as
if they're entitled to perpetual happiness. Schopenhauer, by-product of similarly smugly affluent early
nineteenth-century Germany, believed that

> [w]hat disturbs and depresses young people is
> the hunt for happiness on the firm assumption
> that it must be met with in life. From this arises

constantly deluded hope and so also dissatis-
faction. Deceptive images of a vague happiness
hover before us in our dreams, and we search in
vain for their original. Much would have been
gained if, through timely advice and instruc-
tion, young people could have had eradicated
from their minds the erroneous notion that the
world has a great deal to offer them.

Not surprisingly, as in life, so in death. If we can't
avoid dying (but hold on just a cryogenic minute,
maybe we can: all you need is a lot of money and a little
bit of hope in science to save us and ... yeah, right—the
quintessential Western solution to most problems), we
can at least avoid the subject by treating it as morbidly
taboo or existentially irrelevant and acting as if we're
going to live forever, just like we know we deserve. Such
an intellectually and morally corrosive combination of
almost willful ignorance and flagrant egotism has to
have repercussions.

Even acts of undeniable magnanimity can carry
this narcissistic taint. "Let's Conquer Cancer" is a contemporary catchphrase used in research fundraising
campaigns. One doesn't need to have personally lost
someone to this disease to understand the desire to
assist, in whatever small way, in the prolonging of the

quality of life and the lessening of suffering. Still, if the hubris attached to the concept of "conquering" cancer isn't unsettling enough, then the raging egotism implicit in such an ambition certainly is. Diseases like cancer aren't evolutionary aberrations, aren't malevolent mistakes nature has somehow committed—they serve a clear biological purpose, particularly when it comes to the infirm and the aged. If cancer *was* wiped out and life expectancy among the elderly suddenly soared by, say, even just five years, the already grossly overpopulated planet would be severely burdened (ecologically, economically, and otherwise) by millions more still-ailing (no matter how much fundraising gets done, there'll never be a cure for death) and increasingly age-incapacitated human beings. Life-ending diseases like cancer are simply doing their evolutionary job, making way for the new by eliminating the old. "The aim of all life is death," Freud wrote in *Beyond the Pleasure Principle*. To wish it otherwise is not only irrational, but selfish.

It also might be unnatural. Contra the specious, so-called "argument from desire" (essentially, all human desires have real objects that exist in relation to these same desires, so if human beings throughout history have longed to believe in a personal, eternity-granting God, then some kind of personal, eternity-granting God must therefore exist), Freud posited that, at our deepest, most subterranean level of consciousness, we desire not eternal life, but obliteration, what he referred to in *Beyond the Pleasure Principle* as the "sublime necessity" of our return to an inorganic state.

Occasionally, this desire can even be detected peeking past the subconscious. Here's Madame de Lieven, a nineteenth-century French noblewoman (once courted by George IV), writing from the luxurious Brighton Pavilion to her lover about an experience she'd had while sitting on a seaside rock and reading Byron's mopey masterpiece, *Childe Harold*:

> I always took the poem with me when I went to sit on a certain rocky point, which is quite dry at low tide, but completely submerged at high. Lord Byron says terrible and sublime things about death by drowning... I was reading it one day on the rocks; and I felt that nothing could be simpler than to stay on the point until the sea had covered it. I conceived the idea quite dispassionately. I cannot help believing... that we all have a certain tendency to madness... Evidently, my hour of madness had come. I experienced... nothing but a great unconcern in my heart and in my head. I waited on the

rock a good half-hour...but the tide did not
rise. When at last it did, my madness had ebbed
as the water advanced.

I've always admired those individuals who consciously and devotedly used themselves up, the ones
Kerouac was talking about in *On the Road* who burned,
burned, and burned. I want my rock stars dead young,
my athletes injured often, my artists and writers as
willing to sacrifice their corporeal selves in the pursuit
of aesthetic bliss (for the benefit of both themselves
and others) as dedicated soldiers advancing up a hill.
(Like the novelist Jean Rhys, for instance, who claimed
that if she worked and lived any less intensely, she
would not have "earned her death.") "Wedged as we
are between two eternities of idleness," Anthony Burgess
wrote in his memoir *Little Wilson and Big God*, "there is
no excuse for being idle now."

Everyday acts of conspicuously choosing height-
ened experience and enjoyment over simple survival
are just as compelling and inspiring, as when Freud
writes to his doctor, who'd strongly suggested he give
up his cherished cigars for the benefit of his overall
health, "I am not observing your ban on smoking. Do
you think it is such a glorious fate to live so many years
in misery?" Later, battling jaw cancer, when he does

temporarily extinguish his stogie, he writes to the same physician, "For six days now I have not smoked a single cigar, and it cannot be denied that I owe my well-being to this renunciation. But it is sad." Death is sad, too, obviously, but, being something we ultimately can't avoid, is less depressing than a misspent life, something we *do* have some control over. "The advantage of living is not measured by length," Montaigne wrote, "but by use; some men have lived long, and lived little; attend to it while you are in it."

Assuredness and contentedness are enjoyable, if necessarily fleeting states (and more enjoyable for being so), but not attributes upon which to construct an enriching, invigorating personal philosophy. Children need to feel safe and secure in order to grow into emotionally healthy, confident adults; once grown to adulthood, however, to continue to base one's existence on a foundation of comfort, security, and consolation is to retard further emotional and intellectual growth. Crudely put, it's safer, but it's not nearly as interesting or as stimulating.

Tragedy is not supposed to make one feel assured and content. The character Savage in Aldous Huxley's *Brave New World* says, "I don't want comfort. I want God, I want poetry, I want real danger, I want freedom, I want goodness. I want sin." To which Mustapha

Mond incredulously replies, "In fact, you're claiming the right to be unhappy." Unhappy, perhaps—God can't be known, real poetry is rare, goodness is hard to practise, sin is difficult to avoid and to live with—but potentially more fulfilled. Acknowledging Montaigne's claim that "Death is the condition of your creation, it is part of you; you are fleeing from your own selves [if you believe—and act—otherwise]" is the single most important part of a tragic vision of life.

Carpe diem, life is not a dress rehearsal, *la la la la* live for today: everybody knows it, even everyone who doesn't do it anyway. But seizing the day isn't so simple after age forty. Up to that point, making the best of the time you're allotted in life is commensurate with what gibbering, grasping, gluttonous youth does instinctively anyway: gobble down the good stuff, hunt down new stuff that might be good too, and never forget to remember that tonight might be the night, this movie/book/music could be the greatest movie/book/music you've ever seen/read/heard, and this person might not just be some-body but might just be the one (or at least one of them). Mostly they're not, of course, although sometimes they are, give thanks, and it's all a panting part of the race to get to who you're supposed to be. And if you're lucky, you do. Race completed. Game over. The end.

Except it's not: it's only halftime and you're a new-trick-challenged old dog and this is what you like and what you don't like and these are the people who people your little self-made world and tonight will likely be a lot like last night, just like tomorrow will probably be just like today. Only one life to live and you've already lived it, and with a few more déjà vu decades still left to go.

One solution is to keep behaving and believing as if you're still on the good side of middle-age. Keenly pursuant of new experiences, new people, new ideas, new challenges—it's almost as if you were twenty again and the world was still dewy new. And sometimes it works. For a while. Most times, though, when it's not merely diverting, it's downright pathetic (man leaves wife for much younger woman because she makes him "feel alive" again—until she doesn't anymore; woman chucks it all to finally write the book she always knew she had inside her—turns out it wasn't there after all). If everything really does have its season, then passionate desire and exhilaration belong to the spring and summer months of life's calendar, when curiosity, strength, and resilience are also in their warm and summery prime.

Walking into a bookstore or a record shop when I was young used to feel like anything could happen, that my life could be changed forever by the discovery of a single new-to-me author or musician. It was as if unknown books and records were waiting for me to discover them and let them teach me, enlighten me, transform me. And frequently they did, too. You are what you read and listen to and look at.

Then I read and listened to everything there was to read and hear. This is a slight exaggeration. What happened was, I became a writer and began to consume less as I came to produce more. After three or four hours of throwing down and moving around words on the page, my appetite for consuming someone else's efforts waned. (My wife, a painter, reads about two books for every one that I do. It makes sense.) I still frequent book and record stores, but, more often than not, it's like I'm a hockey card-trading kid again: *Got it, got it, got it*. It's a happy—and rare—day when I can say, *Need it*.

This used to bother me. As good as I believed my life was, and as much as I appreciated everyone and everything that helped me construct such a life, there still remained this feeling of, *Yes, but is that all there is? Is the best part—the most exhilarating part—over?* Kerouac the man provides an example of what can happen when someone outlives the values of an earlier self and doesn't or can't cultivate new ones. The quest—for new experiences, places, people, mores—is the key to understanding not just Kerouac's work, but his own self-identification, where all of life's confusion, suffering, and failure is redeemed by the sacred search for more, to go further, to break on through. What a surprise, then—what a crushing, debilitating surprise—to discover that you're fat, alcoholic, bored, middle-age, and living with your mother. Kerouac's solution was to drink more and talk louder and act more outrageously, all in a sad, desperate impersonation of his younger, genuinely rapacious self. I need a new kind of kick, the Cramps sang. Kerouac did, too, but unfortunately he never discovered any.

It's not only legendary drunks like Kerouac who increasingly rely on alcohol and/or drugs to evoke a less time-burdened, more excitable, more spirited self. The artificial energy supplied by booze and other less legal intoxicants can't help but tantalize anyone whose body is slowing down and whose mind sometimes feels as if it's been there, done that, many, many times already. The busy businessman or businesswoman revitalized after a couple of before-dinner martinis. The exhausted housewife or househusband—the kids finally down for the night and the dinner dishes washed and put away and the other half asleep in front of the TV—soothed and sorted by a nice big glass of red wine and a surreptitious cigarette. All of them—all of *us*—knowing that, as Milton wrote, "one sip of this/will bathe drooping spirits in delight." Whatever is lacking in our own chemistry, it's hard not to attempt to rectify with the kind of chemistry one can buy in a bottle or a pill.

I can sympathize. Man, can I sympathize. It really *is* a drag getting old. (And the only thing worse than getting older is not getting older: dying.) A self-image (such as, one needs to still feel/act young even though one isn't) *can* be tyrannical and censorious. Habits *are* hard to break. Drugs and alcohol have a lot to offer humanity, and I've sung their praises in print as loudly as anyone. But even if we do manage to successfully use them to feel younger when we're old or buoyant when we're depressed, too often we feel even older or more depressed the next day. Utilized primarily to obfuscate reality, they're just another lie, like the belief in personal immortality or that death isn't something we need to concern ourselves with because when we're dead we won't care.

Happiness is hard work. Cultivating genuine, lasting happiness isn't as simple as putting wine in your stomach or pot smoke in your lungs. "Virtue will have nothing to do with ease... It demands a steep and thorny road," Montaigne wrote. Altering the way you think and live as you continue to age and change means working hard to learn how to die. But learning how to die also means learning how to live. "Since we cannot change reality," Nikos Kazantzakis wrote, "let us change the eyes which see reality." Death is real. So is growing old. But so is our ability to adapt to each.

I don't celebrate Christmas (I'm not a Christian) or my birthday (I'm not a child) and I don't have any children of my own to help mark the passing of time. One thing I do have, however, is the annual book sales that the various University of Toronto colleges hold every fall. I've been going every year since I was an undergraduate, and although my attendance record isn't perfect, it's good enough for the various book sales to have been a consistent part of my life for more than a quarter of a century. The appearance around campus of posters announcing the Victoria, Trinity, and University College book sales are almost as reliable a reminder that summer is gone and autumn has begun as the drop in temperature and the leaves lying on the ground. A few years ago, they also provided a reminder of a different sort.

One of the virtues of youth is covetousness. More experiences, more different kinds of experiences, more more more. V.S. Pritchett defined genius as "spiritual greed," and the genius of youth is delineated by how much life it can gobble up before it eventually grows tired of chewing. What this means for someone stalking the tables at a second-hand book sale is, naturally, looking for books you want to read, but also books you simply *have* to own. Turned on to the fiction of not-nearly-well-known-enough Wilfred Sheed, how exciting to find a hardcover first edition of his 1961 novel *Square's Progress* for only three dollars, tax included. Eventually—over the course of many years and many more book sales and used bookstore expeditions—your very own half-shelf of Sheed, Wilfred. This is called connoisseurship. And if at that same book sale you manage to discover a nicer copy of Oswald Spengler's *Decline of the West* than the one you already own (still a paperback, but the two volume Windham Press edition), this must be purchased as well. At twenty years old you needed to read it. At thirty it was on the list of books you intended to read. At forty it's a book that, if nothing else, looks impressive on your bookshelf. It doesn't matter if it's becoming less and less likely it'll ever get read—it's an undeniably important book, everybody says so, so you need to have it. (It's the same reason why you're compelled to own the last three volumes of Anthony Powell's *Dance to the Music of Time* even though you've only read the first of these and it was only just okay.) This is called acquisitiveness.

What cooled my completist zeal wasn't that I ran out of room or the names of new titles or authors to collect. It was what was written on the inside page of a paperback collection of Paul Tillich essays I picked up one October afternoon at the Victoria College book sale. In neat, hand-printed blue ink was the name of a recently deceased former professor of mine. Each of the annual book sales are held to help raise money for each respective college's library and scholarship fund, and the book I was holding was clearly a donation from the personal library of my former teacher. He was a philosophy professor, and even the small library in his office at Vic was alternately overwhelming and inspiring to a more than slightly intimidated undergraduate from Chatham, Ontario (population 40,000) asking for clarification on the grade he'd received on his slaved-over, yet still mediocre, essay. And now here was that same professor's library scattered across the room to be picked up, flipped through, and either tossed back on the table or added to the to-be-purchased piles belonging to a bunch of strangers.

But it wasn't the impersonality of the distribution of his beloved books that gave me pause (the money raised from their sale was going to a cause he obviously believed in and the books themselves were ending up in appreciative hands); it was the realization that this was likely the fate of my own books and records and CDs. The first thing I thought of was that old, stupid joke:

you don't buy beer, you just rent it. I was only renting
my books, even the ones that were most prized or had
been most influential for me as a writer or been acquired
with the most effort. As a result, the idea of continuing
the search for volumes four and seven of Will and Ariel
Durant's *History of Civilization*, an eleven-volume collection I'd had plans to read in its entirety since admiring
it in the Chatham Public Library when I was a teenager but which by this point I knew was never going
to happen, suddenly lost its appeal. Acquisition for
the sake of acquisition now seemed foolish. Worse: it
seemed conceited. Whatever impulse fuels the collect-
or's fervour—the quest for personal permanency or
emotional self-completion by accumulative proxy—
was almost entirely extinguished that day.

When all is said and done (you know you're onto
something true when the clichés start cascading
down): [the] size [of your record collection] doesn't
matter; you can't take [those beautiful first editions of
books you're never going to read] with you; death
don't have no mercy [in spite of your brimming library
and extensive vinyl collection]. And acknowledging
these truths made me sad. A little bit frightened, too.
For the majority of my adult life, more meant better.
More books and records indicated more potential
excitement, more incipient growth, more fecund life.

What was I supposed to do now? Stop collecting and just wait around to die? Insight and integrity are wonderful things, but what the hell was I supposed to do with myself for the next twenty-five years?

In time, one answer announced itself: less accumulating and greater familiarity with what I already owned. I had to admit that I could recall more than once in the past coming home with a new book or (more frequently) record only to realize, when I went to file it on the shelf, I already had a copy. It's helpful to be reminded that books and records and CDs are foremost for reading and listening to, and if they do happen to furnish a room or scratch someone's clandestine collector's itch, well, that's just a nice bonus. I began to read what was new to me but already mine, as well as re-reading some of my favourite books. I wouldn't necessarily start from the beginning with the intention of re-reading the entire thing, but would often open the book up to a random page and simply savour the author's voice, any book's DNA and the underlying reason it was a favourite book to begin with. I wasn't able to say I actually "read" book X again—not in the usual sense, anyway—but what I lost in comprehensiveness I gained in a deeper acquaintance with what's most important to me as a reader: the book's personality as manifest in its inimitable prose style.

I also began to divest myself of duplicates of some of my favourite records. In the beginning the idea had been to snatch up extra copies of original pressings whenever I came across them because there were poor unenlightened souls in the world who hadn't heard the Word yet. But after everyone who I thought would "get it" got one gratis, I was often still in possession of multiple copies of seminal LPs like John Hartford's *Mark Twang*, Willie P. Bennett's *Tryin' to Start Out Clean*, and John Stewart's *California Bloodlines*. Magnanimity aside, it was hard to deny how pleasant it felt to hold a fat stack of so much goodness in my hands, to know that all of that aural beauty was mine all mine, to gloat in the reflected glory of such essential art. Then one day it occurred to me: what the hell was my wife going to do with multiple copies of Paul Siebel's *Woodsmoke and Oranges* when I was dead? One copy, yes—"My Town" is one of her favourite sing-a-long sad songs—but three, including a rare white label promo? It took awhile, but I'm almost duplicate free now. (*Almost*—understanding something isn't always the same as knowing it.) The cash I received from selling them made letting them go a little easier, as did the hope that someone else might have a chance to discover something very special for him or herself, just like I had.

In other words, it was less about putting another quantitative notch in my collecting belt and more about qualitatively getting to know my books and music—and me, because that's one of the things good art does—a little bit better. Developing a deeper familiarity with, for example, Virginia Woolf's voice as expressed through her voluminous journals (and, as a consequence, learning how to live with greater determination, healthy self-deprecation, and simple stoicism) was a lesson in slowing down, wanting less, lingering longer. Still, it was impossible to deny the loss of the sense of excitement and adventure that sometimes accompanies a brand new book or record. Then I discovered the Allman Brothers Band.

I'd heard some of their music before, of course—"Melissa" is such a lovely song, anyone can recognize that, and "Ramblin' Man" was top-forty material when I was a kid—but what I really discovered was the sound of Duane Allman's guitar. Ample cynicism is always justified when it comes to anything a politician says or any electric guitar solo exceeding twenty seconds, so my disinterest in the band Duane formed and named after his brother and himself was warranted. But something happened. I don't remember when or where, but somehow I heard something in one of their songs that made me want to listen to more. It must have been a lick, a tone, or something else equally beguiling produced by Duane's scintillating guitar playing, but whatever it was, I was intrigued enough to purchase a used copy of the Allman Brothers' *At Fillmore East*.

From the casual, almost offhand four-second spoken word announcement that starts off side one of the original two-record set—*Okay, the Allman Brothers Band*—to the slide-guitar scream of Duane's 1959 cherry sunburst Les Paul that kicks off opening track "Statesboro Blues," excitement and adventure were back on the agenda. And the seeds of this sonic revelation had been in my record collection all along. The Allmans' sound was rock and roll mixed up with the blues, elements I didn't need anyone to explain to me, but assembled and fused and played in such a way that I was experiencing something I'd never heard before. With the aid of plenty of time, a set of good headphones, and a lot of cheap Portuguese red wine, I came to appreciate not only the driving (that was the rock and roll part), soulful (that was the blues part) genius of Duane-era Allman Brothers music, but something else I hadn't counted on: a curiosity about jazz.

Not because I wanted people to think I was into jazz (my, how cultured he is) or because I was bored and desperate for something new (maybe I'll go online and buy myself a new hobby) or because I thought I might be a neophyte jazz devotee (I grew up listening to rock and roll, and a saxophone could never mean as much to me as an electric guitar—you don't choose the things you love), but because, along with the rock and roll ferocity and the bluesy soulfulness, there was often something else in the Allman Brothers Band, something slippery, searching, swinging, tantalizingly elusive. And appealing. So this is what jazz people are talking about when they say a performer will introduce a musical theme and then explore it, looking for fresh ways to hear it and new places to take it. A little bit of research uncovered Duane's two biggest jazz influences— John Coltrane's *My Favorite Things* and Miles Davis' *Kind of Blue*—and, after picking these two up on CD, I took my first steps toward being not entirely ignorant of jazz as an art form.

And if you listen to Coltrane enough, you can't help but listen to McCoy Tyner, too, his endlessly inventive piano comping not only providing the perfect rhythmic counterpoint to Coltrane's wild saxophone joyrides, but also compelling one to search out Tyner's own solo work, the cornily titled, but melodically rich hard-bop of *The Real McCoy*, for example. As for the magnificently mutable Davis, the long musical metamorphosis that was his career (from be-bop to cool jazz to modal music to jazz-rock to jazz-funk to...) would take a lifetime to digest and understand and fully appreciate. Luckily, I've also discovered several excellent jazz writers (like

Nat Hentoff, Eric Nisenson, Gary Giddins, and John Szwed) to assist me along the way, a whole new field of literature to collect and conquer. Emboldened by my Coltrane and Davis adventures, I've since gone on to investigate (both on CD and through biographies and critical studies) the wonderfully skewed melodicism of Theolonious Monk, the sparkling jazz guitar of Grant Green, the joyful minimalism of Keith Jarrett.

But the magic mongrel music of the Allman Brothers or the teasing beauty of Coltrane's and Davis' and others' inspired playing isn't the point. The point is, I've enjoyed many hours of enlivening music I wouldn't have listened to otherwise, and I look forward to enjoying many, many more. And the impetus for this new interest and pleasure was there all along, I didn't have to go looking for it. Turns out my searching and seeking days aren't over yet.

PART FOUR

Obviously, you haven't got a chance.

The planet is overpopulated and overheating, good jobs are disappearing, murderous imperialism remains unabated, the strong continue to prey upon the weak, bad art and illogicality are routinely praised and prosper, and, oh yeah, you're going to die. Probably not today, likely not tomorrow, but almost certainly sooner than you think. "A stone is a better pillow than many visions," Robinson Jeffers wrote. So grab your favourite rock and say goodnight.

Goodnight, however—not goodbye. Honesty is a cardinal virtue, but despair and quietism are not, and the latter don't necessarily follow from the former. To acknowledge painful truths—whether about the world or oneself—is the first step toward constructing a truly humanistic, authentically happy existence. It's only just that, though—the first step. To periodically sear one's flesh on the flames of unpleasant realities may be unavoidable, but to obsessively pick at the resultant scab is a choice. It's also to remain in a perpetual state of intellectual and emotional adolescence.

Nietzsche was my favourite philosopher as a student because he didn't sound like a philosopher (too eloquent, too witty, too engaging). Perhaps this should have been my clue that it might have been a good idea to switch majors. Instead, I completed my degree, but began to view philosophers less as objective truth tellers and more as secret autobiographers, the world as they described it clearly reminiscent of their own inner world. Albert Camus made this very point, claiming that "The philosopher, even if he is Kant, is a creator. He has his characters, his symbols, and his secret action. He has his plot endings...The *Ethics* itself, in one of its aspects, is but a long and reasoned personal confession." This didn't mean, however, that there wasn't a lot to be learned from a philosopher's admittedly particularized vision of reality; in fact, the less pseudo-scientific and all-encompassing the verdict, and the more unabashedly individual the vision (as was the case with, among a few others, Nietzsche, Kierkegaard, Marcel, and Schopenhauer), the more intellectually malleable and useful this vision seemed to be. One of the many splendid virtues of stories, whether they are experienced via literature, films, religious narratives, societal myths, or philosophical disquisitions, is that they help the individual better see and therefore understand his or her own life (so often such a frustratingly opaque thing). And because there can be no real happiness without real understanding, stories—in whatever form one finds them—are essential to living a good life.

As an earnest undergraduate—is there any other kind?—Nietzsche's parable "On the Three Metamorphoses" ("how the spirit became a camel; and the camel, a lion; and the lion, finally, a child") contained in *Thus Spake Zarathustra* was revelatory. Of course it was. What could have been more attractive to a proudly self-exiled, working-class suburbanite than Nietzsche's exhortation to "feed…on the acorns and grass of knowledge and, for the sake of the truth, suffer…hunger in one's soul"? Raised in a culture of suffocating material voracity and somnambulistic complacency and stultifying conformity, to embrace ruthless honesty as one's guiding ethic seemed nothing less than heroic. (Who needed to be a bruising hockey player when one could be a ruthless truth-seeker?) Nietzschean heroism isn't mere martyrdom to unpleasant realities like inevitable personal extinction, however. After one has, camel-like, taken on the heavy burden of truth-seeking (and truth-accepting), one has two additional obligations.

First, it's necessary to exhibit leonine aggression and reject the stale and superficial (if admittedly comforting) values inherited from one's society or the fantasies manufactured by one's subconscious. The human species would seem to prefer illusion to reality, and that's why we so readily flock to the consoling myths of philosophy, religion, societal fables, and simple self-delusion. Pain—whether physical or mental—is unpleasant, and human beings tend to do whatever they can to avoid it. And who can condemn, for instance, someone repressing memories of early sexual abuse? An animal doesn't have to be convinced that pain is a bad thing to be circumvented, and before we're anything else, we're animals. But—at our best—we're more than that, too, and avoidance of disagreeable truths, if certainly understandable, is both ignoble and ultimately counterproductive. "They live ill who expect to live always," wrote the first-century Roman dramatist Publius Syrus. What is repressed doesn't go away, and when it does surface, as it usually does, its impact is amplified. Morally and pragmatically, it pays to tell the truth.

Second, it's necessary to go beyond rejecting reassuring values and consoling lies, and imperative that we "assume the right of new values," something "that is the most terrifying assumption for a reverent spirit that would bear much." Terrifying, because to impotently resign oneself to full-time indifference or nihilism is to foredoom oneself to an unfulfilling existence, one bereft of the final goal of personhood: the celebration of life. To be a celebrator of existence, however, and not a mere scoffer, one needs to aspire to the soul of the child. And the child, Nietzsche argued, "is innocence and forgetting, a new beginning, a game, a self-propelled wheel, a first movement, a sacred 'Yes.' For the game of creation, my brothers, a sacred 'Yes' is needed: the spirit now wills his own will, and he who had been lost to the world now conquers his own soul." Jerry Garcia of the aptly named Grateful Dead, told an interviewer, "Instead of making something that lasts forever...I think I'd rather have fun." *Serious* fun. Fun you're willing to bet your life on.

Committing to full consciousness; rejecting false and unfulfilling values (societal myths; empty consumerism; religious and political fundamentalism; chemically and technologically assisted escapism; et cetera)—existence eventually becomes focused upon searching for, locating, and actively cultivating core chosen values and experiences, ideas and actions that will give one's life real and sustained meaning. Like a new attitude toward death.

When Hamlet pronounces, "What a piece of work is a man, how noble in reason, how infinite in faculties, in form and moving, how express and admirable in action, how like an angel in apprehension, how like a god! the beauty of the world; the paragon of animals; and yet to me, what is this quintessence of dust? Man delights not me; no, nor woman neither," there's really not much to say in response except, "Yep, that's about it." Except that one is also compelled to say much the same thing when Pascal argues in his *Pensées* that

> [m]an is only a reed, the frailest thing in nature; but he is a thinking reed. It is not required that the whole universe should arm itself to crush him; a breath of wind, a drop of water is sufficient to destroy him. But were the universe to crush him, man would still be nobler than that which slays him. For he knows that he dies and that the universe has the better of him. But the universe knows nothing of this.

And what did wise Heraclitus say about such existential paradoxes? "Out of discord comes the fairest harmony."

Bertrand Russell, the same man, you'll recall, who avowed that "when I die I shall rot, and nothing of my ego will survive" and "I should scorn to shiver with terror at the thought of annihilation" also said to a friend, not long before he died at age 97, "I do so hate to leave this world." This mix of dejection and defiance isn't contradictory. Or, if it is, it's an incongruity that's consistent with the paradoxical human condition itself. Truth and sorrow. Which is an excellent description of tragedy. And of human life.

But to say that human life is tragic isn't the same as claiming that the living of it is as well. "The years are tragic but the days are jubilant," Edith Wharton wrote. And until the years we've been allowed are gone, we have the days, jubilant or not. Leopold Bloom, in *Ulysses*, melancholically musing to himself at an acquaintance's funeral, finally rouses himself with the thought that "Plenty to see and hear and feel yet. Feel live warm beings near you. Let them sleep in their maggoty beds. They are not going to get me this innings. Warm beds: warm fullblooded life."

Yes.

EPILOGUE:
Denver, Colorado, East Colfax Ave., 2:44 p.m.

Until fairly recently, the closest I came to dying—and knowing it—was a rainy fall day in the late-1980s. The professor of the philosophy course in which I was enrolled had assigned a chapter from an out-of-print book of which there were only two copies in the entire University of Toronto library system. I can't recall the title of the book or the name of the professor or even the subject of the course, but I do remember feeling, despite the inconvenience of having to check the volume out of the St. Michael's College library and get the chapter photocopied and the volume returned to the library before the two-hour borrowing period had elapsed, as if I was climbing another rung on the academic experience ladder. The three dollars in photocopying fees were worth feeling like a busy, bothered scholar.

I also remember that by the time I'd finished my photocopying at a shop on College Street (where it was three cents a page cheaper than at the university library) it was raining hard—thundering and lightning, too—but

I had neither an umbrella (I was twenty-one or twenty-two years old—what kind of twenty-one or twenty-two year-old owns their own umbrella?) nor the time to wait out the storm. Most library fines were a nickel or a dime a day, but this one was a dollar an hour. What if I wanted to save up and buy an umbrella some day?

I crossed College Street and onto campus, past the Sigmund Samuel library and University College and Hart House, and stood on the curb waiting for the traffic to slow down so I could cut across the busy road to Queen's Park. It was early fall, but the weather wasn't anywhere near autumn fresh—was warm and muggy, the rain not feeling like what rain was supposed to feel like at that time of year (other than watery)—and the cars kept coming, their tires on the wet blacktop like bacon in a greasy pan, so I stayed where I was, waiting for a lull in traffic. Waiting and getting wetter and wetter and worried that I'd be late returning the book (for now, thankfully still dry in my bag). There weren't any traffic lights, and a student had been hit by a car attempting to cross near this spot the year before, but I was ready to risk it if only the parade of automobiles would thin out and slow down just for a moment.

Finally, I saw my chance. I stepped off the curb and inched into the road, just one more car to go and then I'd make my move. Squirrels did it every day, so why not me? Except that the car I was waiting on was going slower than I'd anticipated. I cursed the man behind the wheel of the lagging car for having the temerity to travel five miles below the speed limit and stepped back onto the curb. Then, without thinking about it, stepped right back off and played Pac Man with the trail of fresh cars until I was across the road and standing on Queen's Park grass. How did the wannabe-scholar cross the road? Why, he ran, of course. I congratulated myself on my initiative and started down the path to St. Mike's library, on the other side of the park.

I'd walked maybe five steps when it thundered again, and—*craacckk*—a bolt of lightning struck the tall maple tree just a few feet ahead of me on the path. Decibel-wise, I'd probably heard louder at any number of rock concerts while standing too close to the speakers, but this noise was different. You could *feel* it. It felt *heavy*. This sound was *serious*. I could not only see the long, trunk-length scar the lightning had created, I could smell the sappy smoke wafting upward through the rain. I looked around, and there was no one there, no one had heard or seen what I had. That's when I realized that if that one car hadn't slowed me down, hadn't made me hesitate for the ten seconds or so that it had, I would have been ten seconds or so farther down the path when the lightning blasted the tree. Which might have—probably would have—also blasted me. For years afterward, whenever I was in the park, I'd make a point of looking at the tree. The gash healed over and the tree lived, but its ten-foot-long wound was permanent.

Food for fatal thoughts. Gentle, autumnal ruminations throughout the succeeding decades regarding life's staggeringly capricious fragility. No kidding, seriously, for real. As much as such reflection *can* be real when contemplating something—something like your own death—so seemingly fantastic. And, as said, for a long time, also the closest I'd come to dying and knowing it.

As with most instances of bad luck, the next time something similar occurred, many years later, things couldn't have been better. For one thing, the majority of my next book, a novel, had been written. For me, the compositional sweet spot is being approximately sixty percent of the way through a first draft of a new project. The heavy lifting is done—for the most part, you know what the book is about; you've got a pretty good idea of how it ends; you even have a line on how long it's going to be—and the rest is mainly paying attention to what the story wants to be and how it needs to be told. Something else that's sweet is having a book on the go when you're about to publish an entirely different one. The imminent appearance of the latter is always fun (seeing the finished copy for the first time; reading reviews; touring around and meeting readers), but the inevitable disappointment (finding the first typo; reading reviews; events where there are more authors on the stage than people in the audience) is dissipated somewhat by knowing that there's something else in your life that you do have some control over. The joy of a book-in-progress isn't dependent on other people or good fortune; happiness is as simple as sitting down and opening up your laptop and writing a good sentence. A book on-the-go means having somewhere to hide.

In this case, the new book was in the pre-publication publicity stage, and I was in Denver for a gathering of the American Booksellers Association, a group of independent U.S. booksellers who meet with publishers and writers who have forthcoming books. I was promoting *Lives of the Poets (with Guitars)*, as well as enjoying a paid vacation in an interesting city I'd never been to. I'd done my online pre-trip research like a good tourist should and had a list of Denver's best second-hand book and record stores. I was only hoping that a few of them would be as good as advertised.

For the most part, they were, and one in particular exceeded expectations, having not only a substantial Allman Brothers section, but a separate retail subdivision reserved entirely for just live Allman Brothers concerts, the ideal way to experience the original band's charging, improvisatory brilliance. In spite of the malnourished Canadian dollar, I filled up on the store's offerings and strolled back to the hotel with a big red plastic bag full of assorted CDs, LPs, and books. Also contributing to the jump in my step was the wonderful, spring-like weather (late January fourteen degrees Celsius and blue and bright), the view (look up from the sidewalk to the west and there they were, the Rockies), and the advanced reader's copy of *Lives of the Poets (with Guitars)* tucked into the bag holding my stash of new books and music. I'd seen it for the first time only the day before, and its sheen was still fresh. The walk to the farthest record store was about an hour straight down East Colfax Avenue, and on the return to the hotel I'd stopped for lunch at a diner where I read the *Denver Post* sports page while periodically pulling the ARC out of the bag for quick peeks of admiration. I knew it was silly—it was my tenth book, I knew it would be just the marked-up and discarded advanced reader's copy soon enough—but right now, it didn't feel silly. It felt great, actually. *I* felt great.

The only way I was going to feel even better was by going back to the hotel and having a good workout in the fitness centre followed by a shower and a shave before the evening's events. I was about fifteen minutes away from the Sheraton when, approaching a Popeye's Chicken restaurant, I heard four rapid pops—*pop pop pop pop*—coming from the other side of the building. My first thought was: *Sounds like gunshots.* Then: *People always say that when they hear firecrackers or a car backfiring.* Then I didn't think anything, just watched a young man stagger around the side of the building holding his neck, saying—sounding more surprised than angry or in pain—"I'm shot." It wasn't until the man reeled past me on the sidewalk, still holding his neck, that I realized that those *had* been gunshots I'd heard. By now, a group of five or six people had materialized on the sidewalk, all of us standing near the door of the restaurant, when an elderly woman pushed me out of the way with her shoulder and an "Excuse me, *please*!" and jammed open the glass door with the aid of her cane and disappeared inside. Then we all got the identical idea—safety, sanctuary, refuge—and hurriedly did the same.

All of the customers already inside were either lying or squatting on the floor, and when the kneeling manager saw the influx of new people, he shouted, "Everyone get down below window level!" The frightened faces everywhere I looked were oddly comforting; what I was suddenly most terrified of seeing was what you too-often read about in the newspaper or see on the news: a camouflaged, angry white man with an assault rifle in Anywhere, U.S.A, intent on slaughtering as many people as possible for no explicable reason. If *only* this was a case of one person shooting somebody else. Retrospective sagacity aside, all I can actually remember thinking at the time was one thing: *Things like this don't happen to people like me. I don't deserve this. This shouldn't be happening to me.*

The silence was broken by someone on the other side of the room muttering something I didn't pick up and someone else saying "Here?" and the other person answering "*Right* here. The drive-through. That glass is all busted." It was like that horror movie from when I was kid: *The call is coming from inside the house!* Whoever had fired the four shots had been aiming at someone in line in the drive-through of the restaurant, the same restaurant we'd taken shelter inside. Everyone rose to their feet and briskly walked back out the same door we'd previously scrambled through. The old woman who'd pushed past me getting inside said, "I'm sorry about before." I just nodded.

Out on the sidewalk I still felt scared, but liberated. I walked, not ran—the same as everyone else—in the direction I'd been travelling when I first heard the shots. I was the only one of us going uptown. I was slightly surprised to see the plastic bag still in my hand.

After walking for a couple of minutes, I noticed the weather: the warmth and the sunshine and the cool breeze. I began to notice people, too, people sitting on benches smoking or talking on their phones or eating their lunches, and a large man walking his small dog, and a group of three teenagers wordlessly playing Hacky Sack with great concentration. One of the kids made a diving save with his foot, kept the sack in the air for someone else to kick, and they all laughed and hooted in appreciation. I heard the sound of a siren coming from somewhere. I knew where it was headed.

NOTES

INTRODUCTION

free, oral, informal, personal, Michel de Montaigne, *The Complete Essays of Montaigne*, trans. Donald Frame (Stanford University Press, 1968), vi.

To cheer the gloom, James Thomson, *The Seasons* (A.S. Burns and Burr, 1860), 287.

[S]omeone might say of me, Montaigne, *The Complete Essays of Montaigne*, 808.

good for good people, Mary McCarthy, *Memoirs of a Catholic Girlhood* (Harcourt, Brace and Company, 1957), 23.

To know how to, Montaigne, *The Complete Essays of Montaigne*, 274.

PART ONE

Whenever we attempt to, Lirian Razinsky, *Freud, Psychoanalysis and Death* (Cambridge University Press, 2013), 61.

Everybody has got to, Aram Saroyan, *Last Rites: The Death of William Saroyan as Chronicled by His Son* (William Morrow & Company, 1982), 175.

Paint, not the object, Rosina Neginsky, *Symbolism, Its Origins and Its Consequences* (Cambridge Scholars Publishing, 2010), 338.

No reader who doesn't, Flannery O'Connor, *Mystery and Manners: Occasional Prose*, selected and edited by Sally and Robert Fitzgerald (Farrar, Straus and Giroux, 1969), 91.

The existential project of, Martin Heidegger, *Being and Time: A Translation of Sein and Zeit*, trans. Joan Stambaugh (SUNY Press, 1996), 240.

Death is not my, Bernard N. Schumacher, *Death and Mortality in Contemporary Philosophy* (Cambridge University Press, 2010), 98.

They all muddy their, *The Portable Nietzsche*, ed. and trans. Walter Kaufmann (Penguin Books, 1985), 240.

So long as thinkers, Jules Renard, *The Journals of Jules Renard*, ed. and trans. Louie Borgan and Elizabeth Roget (Tin House, 2008), 169.

When a man takes, Charles Baudelaire, *The Intimate Journals*, trans. Chistopher Isherwood (City Lights Books, 1983), 27.

It might make one, Isabel Constance Clarke, *Shelley and Byron* (Ardent Media, 1971), 122.

In his youth, everybody, Robert Seidenberg and Hortence S. Cochrane, *Mind and Destiny: A Social Approach to Psychoanalytic Theory* (Syracuse University Press, 1964), 107.

Belief in the existence, Simone Weil, *Gravity and Grace*, trans. Emma Crawford and Mario von der Ruhr (Routledge Classics, 2002), 64.

The smaller the mind, Aesop, *The Big Book of Aesop's Fables,* ed. M. Scott Buck (Lulu.com, 2004), 92.

Where be your gibes? William Shakespeare, *The Riverside Shakespeare* (Houghton Mifflin Company, 1974), 1179.

The syllogism he had, Leo Tolstoy, *The Death of Ivan Ilyich and Other Stories,* trans. J.D. Huff and Aylmer Maude (Signet, 1960), 131.

Love does not consist, Antoine de Saint-Exupery, *Airman's Odyssey* (Houghton Mifflin Harcourt, 1943), 195.

The soul selects her, Emily Dickinson, *The Complete Poems* (Little, Brown and Company, 1960), 143.

It is not enough, Wilfred Sheed, *The Good Word & Other Words* (Dutton, 1978), 17.

Whatever can happen at, John L. Bowman, *A Reference Guide to Stoicism: A Compilation of the Principle Stoic Wrings on Various Topics* (Author House, 2014), 37.

He who would teach, Montaigne, *The Complete Essays of Montaigne*, 62.

Let us only listen, Ibid, 822.

PART TWO

And what I assume, Walt Whitman, *Leaves of Grass and Selected Prose* (The Modern Library, 1950), 23.

In our sad condition, *1001 Unforgettable Quotes About God, Faith, and the Bible*, ed. Ron Rhodes (Harvest House Publishers, 2011), 72.

I expect no very, *Bartlett's Book of Quotations*, ed. Clifton Fadiman and Andre Bernard (Little, Brown and Company, 2000), 484.

Nobody thinks of giving, John Morley, *The Works of Voltaire: A Biographical Critique of Voltaire* (Werner, 1905), 272.

everybody is born either, William Robert Wians, *Aristotle's Philosophical Development: Problems and Prospects* (Rowman & Littlefield, 1996), 1.

[i]t is true, there, Friedrich Nietzsche, *Human, All Too Human*, trans., R.J. Hollingdale (Cambridge University Press, 1996), 15.

If you were to, Anthony Mlikotin, *Western Philosophical Systems in Russian Literature: A Collection of Critical Studies* (University of Southern California Press, 1979), 63.

Religion consists in believing, Cesare Pavese, *This Business of Living* (Transaction Publishers, 1964), 105.

the only psychologist from, George H. Smith, *Atheism* (AnVi OpenSource Knowledge Trust, 1974), 472.

Freedom is the recognition, N.D. Arora and S.S. Awasthy, *Political Theory and Political Thought* (Har-Anand Publications, 2007), 152.

the thing with feathers, Dickinson, *The Complete Poems*, 116.

If all the world, Shakespeare, *The Riverside Shakespeare*, 851.

Imagine life without death, Renard, *The Journals of Jules Renard*, 234.

For all the happiness, *Oxford Treasury of Sayings and Quotations*, ed. Susan Ratcliffe (Oxford University Press, 2011), 200.

kind nature's signal of, David Hopkins and Charles Martindale, *The Oxford History of Classical Reception in English Literature: Volume Three (1160–1790)* (Oxford University Press, 2012), 112.

Pale death, with impartial, Horace, *Horace: The Odes, Epodes, Satires, and Epistles*, trans. Various (Frederick Warne & Co., 1889), 10.

Call no man happy, Mary Margaret Mackenzie, *Plato on Punishment* (University of California Press, 1981), 93.

Accustom yourself to believing, Anthony F. Falikowski, *Experiencing Philosophy* (Prentice Hall, 2003), 95.

Loss is nothing else, Frank McLynn, *Marcus Aurelius: A Life* (Da Capo, 2009), xiii.

I do not fear, Trevor Treharne, *How to Prove God Does Not Exist: The Complete Guide to Validating Atheism* (Universal-Publishers, 2012), 74.

It is better to, Andres Sofroniou, *Moral Philosophy, from Socrates to the 21st Aeon* (PsySys, 2010), 157.

Self pity is easily, Elisha O. Ogbonna, *Mastering the Power of Your Emotions: How to Control What Happens in You Irrespective of What Happens to You* (Friesen Press, 2014), 145.

And a handful of, Sophocles, *The Antigone of Sophocles*, trans. Dudley Fitts and Robert Fitzgerald (Harcourt Brace, 1939), 41.

The truth is that, Evelyn Waugh, *The Letters of Evelyn Waugh* (Ticknor and Fields, 1980), 627.

The rational man may, Sheed, *The Good Word & Other Words*, 69.

No more games. No, Shaun Usher, *Letters of Note: An Eclectic Collection of Correspondence Deserving of a Wider Audience* (Chronicle Books, 2014), 64.

I am going to the, Andrew Motion, *Philip Larkin: A Writer's Life* (Faber and Faber, 1993), 521.

[W]hen we are led, Montaigne, *The Complete Essays of Montaigne*, 63.

Nature lends us her, Ibid.

But our machines have, Sherwin B. Nuland, *How We Die: Reflections on Life's Final Chapter* (Vintage Books, 1994), 44.

PART THREE

It must require an, Heinrich Heine, *Pictures of Travel: 1828* (John W. Lovell, 1891), 289.

you become aware that, Renard, *The Journals of Jules Renard*, 242.

When I went in for, Huffington Post, "Wilko Johnson on his terminal cancer: 'Game of Thrones' star says he feels 'vividly alive'" 01/25/2013

I was supposed to be, The Telegraph, "Wilko Johnson remains clear of cancer: The former Dr. Feelgood guitarist has made a remarkable recovery from a terminal diagnosis" 07/05/2015

Death is the normal, Renard, *The Journals of Jules Renard*, 257.

[w]hat disturbs and depresses, Arthur Schopenhauer, *Parega and Paralipomena: Short Philosophical Essays, Volume 1,* trans. E.F.J. Payne (Clarendon Press, 1974), 480.

I always took the, Peter Quennell, *The Pursuit of Happiness* (Little, Brown and Company, 1988), 60–61.

earned her death, Penelope Fitzgerald, *The Afterlife: Essays and Criticism* (Counterpoint, 2003), 223.

I am not observing, Peter Gay, *Freud: A Life for Our Time* (W.W. Norton Company, 1998), 77.

For six days now, Heinz Politzer, *Freud and Tragedy* (Ariadne Press, 2006), 79.

The advantage of living, Montaigne, *The Complete Essays of Montaigne*, 67.

Death is the condition, Ibid, 65.

One sip of this, John Milton, *The Poetical Works of John Milton: With Notes of Various Authors* (Longman and Company, 1826), 379.

Since we cannot change, *Wisdom for the Soul: Five Millennia of Prescriptions for Spiritual Healing*, edited by Larry Chang (Gnosophia Publishers, 2006), 113.

spiritual greed, V.S. Pritchett, *The Complete Essays* (Chatto & Windus, 1991), 784.

PART FOUR

The philosopher, even if, Albert Camus, *The Myth of Sisyphus and Other Essays*, trans. Justin O'Brien (Vintage Books, 1955), 74.

They live ill who, *The Moral Sayings of Publius Syrus, A Roman Slave*, trans. D. Lyman (L.E. Barnard & Company, 1856), 44.

Instead of making something, Amir Bar-Lev, *Long Strange Trip: The Untold Story of the Grateful Dead*, DVD.

Out of discord comes, *The Presocratics* (Bobbs-Merrill Educational Publishing, 1983), edited by Philip Wheelwright, 77.

I do so hate, Ronald Clark, *The Life of Bertrand Russell* (Jonathan Cape, 1975), 637.

The years are tragic, Wilfred Sheed, *Essays in Disguise* (Knopf, 1990), xi.

ALSO BY RAY ROBERTSON:

Home Movies
Heroes
Moody Food
Mental Hygiene: Essays on Writers and Writing
Gently Down the Stream
What Happened Later
David
Why Not? Fifteen Reasons to Live
I Was There the Night He Died
Lives of the Poets (with Guitars)
1979